Day Hikes
of the
Santa Barbara Foothills

Raymond Ford, Jr.

McNally & Loftin, Publishers

© Raymond Ford, Jr. 1984
McNally & Loftin, Publishers
5390 Overpass Road
Santa Barbara, California 93111

Printed and Bound by
Kimberly Press, Inc.
Goleta, California

Third Revised Edition
Second Edition, 1979, was published by
Earthling Bookshop, Santa Barbara

Library of Congress Cataloging in Publication Data

Ford, Raymond, 1943-
    Day hikes of the Santa Barbara foothills.

    Bibliography: p.
    1. Hiking—California—Santa Barbara Region—Guide-
books. 2. Santa Barbara Region (Calif.)—Description and
travel—Guide-books. I. Title.
GV199.42.C22S3194 1984   917.94'91   84-10027
ISBN 0-87461-056-7 (pbk.)

INTRODUCTION

There is something special about the Santa Ynez Mountains. It isn't something that rushes out at you and captures you, like the immediacy of a Yosemite scene or the awe-inspiring silence of the lip of the Grand Canyon. It is not a beauty that floods into the consciousness upon first contact.

It is subtle. Sublime. Something that grows with age and from many experiences. The secret is in spending time—lots of it—on the mountain wall.

This country forces a reorientation of one's perspective to a different standard of beauty. On the surface it seems inhospitable, almost a rude sort of land. But chaparral country has its own beauty, a beauty that develops from within, from heightening one's own senses.

In rewriting *Day Hikes* I have tried to capture some of this feeling, and as such this third edition is both a guide to the trails and an interpretation of the meaning of the Santa Ynez Mountains for myself.

It is also written as an encouragement for you to explore them for yourself, to experience them to their fullest. In the canyons and the trails, the bedrock, and the chaparral, and such experiences, is the meaning of these mountains.

Walk along Camino Cielo on a moonlit evening, or have a snowball fight at Knapp's Castle some February afternoon after storm's end. Take the time to learn about the geologic formations, the backbones of this country, and the immense variety of shrubs, herbs, insects, and animals native to these mountains. Listen to the sound of the wind in the trees, the water splashing against the rocks, and take a plunge in one of the many pools. Let the aroma of the chaparral wash over you as you lie back on the bedrock after the swim. Then it will grow on you as well.

But please, take a wilderness morality with you at all times. Take your garbage out with you, and make an effort to leave the Santa Ynez Mountains in better condition than you found them. They will stay only as wild and beautiful as you leave them.

DEDICATION

To Kathleen
Who will be with me
Always,
And who one day
I hope
Will be with me.

TABLE OF CONTENTS

CHAPTER ONE

THE MOUNTAIN WALL

It is the sound of one particular canyon I remember best. The walls are steep and narrow, the pools clear and crisp, and overhead thick clusters of alder filter the sunlight, creating a soft green cathedral-like setting. But the unfettered splashings of the creek and the callings of unseen songbirds in the brush that draw me back time and again. It is a world apart, just a few miles from the heart of the city. Though it is barely fifteen minutes from my doorstep to the trail's edge, the difference is both dramatic and startling.

The canyon rises in staircase fashion through alternating layers of sandstone and shale, and a thin wisp of a trail follows, meandering through scattered groves of oak at some points, switching steeply around headwalls of bedrock at others—into the heat and openness of the chaparral hillsides, then back again into the coolness of the creekside.

The beauty begins immediately, and just a few yards from the road's edge there is sharp delineation between the world being entered and the one left behind. Upstream are the first pools, and the breeze. Light and cool. Airy. Invigorating. The sound catches at me, grabs me, and pushes me on. Farther to the interior are waterfalls, sun-bathing spots, and hidden valleys.

There is one pool I return to often. No trail leads up to it, nor is it marked on a map. But if you explore enough of the Santa Ynez Mountains, you'll find its enchanting grace for yourself. Half the thrill is in the search for such sylvan retreats, the other in the experience of the place. This one has a waterfall above and one below. Inbetween, caught in the midst of the twin towers of water, is a deep pool. Spacious, apple-green in

1

color, and cold even in the summer heat, it is a niche that suits a personal need of mine, to be by myself for awhile.

There are four canyons such as this behind Santa Barbara—Mission, Rattlesnake, Cold Springs and San Ysidro—each with its own unique charm. There are countless others hidden deep in the flank of the Santa Ynez Mountains whose enchanting nature lures me back time and again.

The Chaparral

From the perspective of the city, however, the abruptness of the mountain wall as it rises nearly 4,000 feet to its crest at La Cumbre Peak, the spiny layerings of sandstone, the insipid coloring of the chaparral, combine to convey a sense of inhospitality and dullness. These Santa Ynez Mountains do not appear inviting.

For fifty miles they run unbroken and because of the peculiar way they have been juxtaposed on the countryside in an east-west direction, the sun pours down on their southerly slope at nearly right angles. This scorches all but the hardiest of chaparral plants, and the vegetation that is visible from Santa Barbara survives mainly by adapting to the lack of summer rain and the searing Santa Ana winds with a uniform, colorless appearance.

In addition, the dense chaparral cover gives sense of impenetrability. The thick, interlocking branches and the needle-sharp points of the tough, leathery leaves seem more to say *Keep Out, No Trespassing* than to invite closer inspection. "Meshed and tangled like concertina wire, and mined with rattlesnakes," one writer has said of the chaparral, "it is impossible to penetrate with anything less persuasive than a light tank."

The chaparral is an elfin forest dominated by shrubs seldom more than fifteen feet in height. What it lacks in stature, though, it makes up for in orneriness. It is primarily evergreen, which protects it from becoming desiccated during the long, rainless summer months, and the leaves are tough and leathery, with prickly edges. It is also dry and resinous, which makes it extremely fire-prone, but this imparts its characteristic fragrance as well. It is this curious juxtaposition of opposites, of toughness and delicacy, that marks chaparral country.

Properly speaking, the chaparral has two distinct elements: the coastal sage (also called the mixed chaparral), and the hard chaparral. The coastal sage is the community of low herbaceous shrubs, rarely more than seven feet in height, that borders the canyons of the lower foothills. The small fuzzy leaves of the yerba santa and the purple, black and white sages are predominantly gray in color, but in the springtime the delicate purple buds of the sages and their overwhelming aromas make this soft chaparral community a treat to be sampled again and again.

This softer chaparral is found along the lower elevations of the Santa Ynez Mountains and on the steep shale slopes, which have insufficient soil to support grasses or species of the oak woodland community. Also found in the soft chaparral are California sagebrush, buckwheat, monkey flower, yarrow, and the wonderful bush that exudes a butterscotch aroma: pearly everlasting.

The hard chaparral is composed of the duller green plants, which dominate the higher elevations. These are dense woody shrubs that grow so thickly as to render travel through them nearly impossible, except in the few years after a wildfire. Despite the less-than-appealing aesthetics of this community, its species are well adapted to the poor soil profile, the short rainy season, and the intense summer heat. These plants are like the tough kids on the block—on the surface neither delicate nor beautiful—but well structured for survival here, and in a Darwinian sort of way, there is a grace to these plant types.

The hard chaparral can be subdivided into two groups. The lower half grows to elevations of about 1,500 feet and is sometimes called chamise chaparral or *el camisal*. Though big pod and greenbark ceanothus, sugarbush, and black sage are also found here, the chamise dominates, often in pure stands such as those around Inspiration Point.

The chamise is a member of the rose family and has tiny needlelike leaves that grow in bundles. Its reddish-brown seed pods, which open during the flowering season, remain on the shrubs for much of the following year's season and give chamise chaparral its characteristic rusty color. Studies have shown that the chamise may provide up to 40 percent of the yearly diet of chaparral deer. Also known as greasewood because of its high oil content, the chamise is responsible for the intensity of many of the mountain wildfires.

4

Manzanita and scrub oak are the predominant species of the upper half of the hard chaparral. Others that are found near the crest are the holly-leaf cherry, chaparral pea, toyon, yucca, bush poppy, prickly phlox, and mountain mahogany. The holly-leaf cherry was called *islay* by the Chumash, who harvested it in the fall and ground it into flour for use during winter months.

The name "chaparral" dates to the time when gaunt Spanish cattle roamed the valleys and foothills of the County, their wanderings unimpeded by either barbed wire or concrete. Rousting these half-wild steer from brush-choked canyons was the task of the rugged, hard-riding vaqueros, who protected their legs from the sharp branches and thorns by wearing tough leggings that extended from belt to boots.

The plant that caused the vaqueros the most annoyance was the interior live oak, known scientifically as *Quercus wislizenii*. A similar oak that grows in Spain was called *el chaparro*, and this was the name given to the scrub oak that the Spaniards found in California.

The "al" suffix, added to the root word *chaparro*, which means "the place of", has led to the dense southland brush being called the chaparral, even though today it includes far more than the pockets of scrub oak where the Spanish cattle used to hide out.

This chaparral countryside is a product of a mediterranean climatic system, which is characterized by moderate, moist winters and long, hot, dry summers. Rainfall is generally sparse, about 17 inches per year in Santa Barbara, and often occurs during a few high-intensity winter storms. Summer temperatures often exceed 100° F. and relative humidities are low, often less than 5 per cent.

Plant communities similar to the chaparral grow in several other parts of the world, including the shores of the Mediterranean Sea, central Chile, South Africa, and southwestern Australia. These regions compose about 3 percent of the earth's land surface. All are located on the western borders of continental land masses in a narrow strip between 30° and 45° north latitude. The weather patterns in these areas are dominated by a pressure zone known as the Pacific High. Locally, in the summer, as the Southwest begins to heat up, this mass of warm stable air moves slightly north and inland, deflecting storms originating in the northern latitudes eastward across Washington and Oregon. Only in the winter does the

Pacific High retreat south and seaward and allow storm fronts access to the Southern California coastline.

Summit and Sea

Although the mountain wall does not have the immediate charm of the city's Mission-style architecture nor the mediterranean grace of palm-lined Cabrillo boulevard, it is the Santa Ynez Mountains, as much as the sea, that define the city's character. Even though most think of Santa Barbara as a beach community, it is the mountain wall that sets it apart from other ocean ports on the California coast.

This is a region that is still dominated by the great forces of nature: the jumble of tectonic plates periodically bursting forth with shivers of destruction, the wildfires that defy control, the floods that occasionally destroy homes and steadily usurp the holding capacity of vital County reservoirs. It is these forces that have molded the land, given shape and texture to the Santa Ynez Mountains, and clothed them with a vegetative cover. And despite man's insistence otherwise, it is these that will continue to dominate the land and the city.

There are nine ways over the mountain wall. Three are at the passes: Gaviota, Refugio, and San Marcos, at 2,250 feet the lowest point along the crest. The other six are by trail: the Arroyo Burro, Tunnel, Rattlesnake, Cold Springs, San Ysidro, and Romero. The trails are reminders that for most of its history Santa Barbara has been geographically isolated from the rest of Southern California.

To the south is the ocean. Powerful northern swells funnel around Point Conception and between the Channel Islands, making this a treacherous body of water even today. It was no accident that the *tomol*, the Chumash planked canoe, was the finest seagoing vessel to be found on the California coast.

To the north the Santa Ynez Mountains form the first line of defense against penetration. Beyond are the San Rafael Mountains, the thin edge of Hurricane Deck, and the indomitable Sierra Madres. When Gaspar de Portola led the first Spanish land expedition north from San Diego in 1769, no wonder he opted to follow the coastline around Point Concep-

tion rather than brave the hardship offered by travel through the Santa Barbara mountain ranges.

For me, an occasional hike up Tunnel Trail serves to remind me of the steepness and ruggedness of the mountain wall. The hike up out of Mission Canyon is long and tiring. Above, the sharp upthrust of a massive layer of sandstone, known locally as the Mission Crags, dominates the view and tends to eat away at my confidence. Barely halfway up the mountain wall I already feel the strain of the effort.

"By trail and by brush-bucking," the late Ed Spaulding, Santa Barbara author and educator, used to say, "it is a very weary, weary way and one that tests not only the leg muscles and the lung capacity but the enthusiasm for the out-of-doors as well." Easily crossed by automobile, these mountains cannot be taken so lightly when my legs must provide the locomotion.

The ascent is a slow process, and as I make my way toward the crest what returns most is a sense of time. And of place. At one point I stop and sit on a large, flat sandstone slab, to let my breath return to some semblance of normality. Below, the canyon winds its way toward me like a slender thread of green. Beyond are the foothills, golden yellows that seem to undulate their way to the valley floor. Though my lungs still heave with the effort, I feel both excited and alive.

The wind gusts occasionally, but mostly it whispers across the chaparral like a soft moan. The minty scent of purple sage and the aroma of yerba santa invade my consciousness. Overhead a pair of red-tail hawks soar on an updraft, their screeches letting me know they own this particular piece of the sky. In the distance is the muffled sound of Mission Creek.

Here life decelerates from the twentieth-century pace that has been forced on it. There is time to absorb the small details and to sift through the bits and pieces of this part of the mountain wall.

Nearby where I sit there is a small crease in the bedrock, bone dry now, but filled with the potential, in the winter months, to channel large volumes of water, and with it tons of cobblestones, sands, sands and silt, if not for the chaparral vegetation that covers the mountainside.

The Thirsty Land

Tunnel Trail was built at the turn of the century as a link between a tunnel being bored in the south side of the Santa Ynez Mountains and a dam to be built on the north side, at the Gibraltar Narrows on the Santa Ynez River. In 1900, with a population of barely 6,000 people, Santa Barbara already was experiencing its first water crisis, although earlier Chumash populations must have approached 8,000 in the South Coast area without severely taxing food or water resources.

As early as 1870, when the population was about 2,900, Santa Barbarans had begun to feel the need to develop water supplies. In 1872, local investors organized the Mission Water Company, which tapped the Mission Creek water supply. In 1887, the De La Guerra Water Company was formed and seven artesian wells were drilled to a depth of 200 feet to begin capturing underground supplies. Several years later the two companies were consolidated and became the Santa Barbara Water Company. This company proceeded to buy a 17,000-acre tract in the upper Santa Ynez River, which embraced all potential reservoir sites along this section.

Impetus toward using the Santa Ynez River as a source of water for Santa Barbara grew gradually. A series of dry years in the mid-1890s and a donation to the city of 320 acres in Cold Springs Canyon by Eugene Sheffield helped the process. The city first turned to the Santa Ynez Mountains in January, 1896, when at the elevation of 1,400 feet, Cold Springs Tunnel was carved a mile into the mountain wall, adding some 290 acre-feet of water to the city's annual supply.

After the years 1898, 1899, and 1900 proved to be ones of sustained drought, the city hired J.B. Lippincott, head of the hydrological branch of the U.S. Geological Survey to investigate the possibility of developing water storage facilities on the Santa Ynez River. His recommendation was to construct a tunnel from Mission Canyon through the Santa Ynez Mountains to the Santa Ynez River near the Gibraltar Narrows.

Initial work began in 1904, when Santa Barbara entered a contract with the water company to build the tunnel. However, when the construction crew ran into serious difficulty with sulphur gas, which incapacitated several workers, the city released the contractor and proceeded with the work itself. Additional funds were raised in 1908 and 1910, and in 1912 the tunnel was completed through the mountain.

In 1915, a $590,000 bond issue was passed which authorized the construction of Gibraltar Dam. Construction began in 1918, with materials being transported by a narrow-gauge electrical railroad through the tunnel. The dam was completed in 1920.

A Sense of Perspective

The rock upon which I sit here on Tunnel Trail is known as Coldwater Sandstone. It is Eocene rock, a remnant of a geologic era of some fifty million years ago—ancient when measured against the span of human lives but relatively young on a geologic scale. Rubbing my hand over the rock, I can feel the imbedded shells of prehistoric oyster, which once thrived in the brackish water of the tidal flat. This rock was once part of a seashore environment, perhaps something like that which exists today at Morro Bay.

Above, the switchbacks become more difficult, and as I hike I concentrate more on the trail than the view. Then almost before I realize, the summit is upon me and I am on the crest. Sitting on the top of a large knoll and sipping on the last of a precious quart of water, I absorb the feeling of the Santa Ynez Mountains.

What I feel is a sense of perspective. From here the land appears basically unaltered, despite man's intensive efforts to the contrary over the past two centuries. The valley floor is filled with people now, and the mountains are managed for water, for wildfire, and for wildlife by the Forest Service. But taken as a whole, the dominant feature of the land is still its mountainous, roadless, and essentially primitive character.

Noone has caught the feeling of being up on the crest quite like Stewart Edward White, who wrote The Mountains in 1904:

> "Our favorite route to the main ridge was by a way called the Cold Spring Trail . . . . Beyond the apparent summit you found always other summits yet to be climbed. And all at once, like thrusting your shoulders out of a hatchway, you looked over the top.
>
> "Then came the remarks. Some swore softly; some uttered appreciative ejaculation; some shouted aloud; some gasped; one man uttered three times the word 'OH,'—once in wild enthusiasm, OH! Then invariably they fell silent and looked."

CHAPTER TWO

MY FAVORITE PLACES

Lizard's Mouth is a sliver of bedrock nestled high in the Santa Ynez Mountains west of San Marcos Pass, a place filled with sandstone boulders, underground caves, and water-worn channels that separate huge slabs of rock like pieces of a gigantic puzzle. This is land that has yielded only stubbornly to the forces of nature, a place where one can appreciate and begin to understand the slow pulse of the earth's evolution.

It is a land that has undergone radical changes over the past several hundred million years, including some very dramatic ones in the last three or four million years. The bedrock has shifted, the climate has changed many times, and every earthquake reminds me that the entire process, even today, is in constant flux. The land may remain rigid for the balance of this day perhaps, for the month, the year, or, for that matter, the rest of my life. Nonetheless, it is part of a fluid, on-going process.

I made a very special trip to Lizard's Mouth several years ago. It was in autumn, during Santa Barbara's Indian summer, and the air was warm and moisture-laden. A tropical storm had invaded from the south. From the perch of a small cave, a friend and I sat huddled as we watched dark billowing clouds head our way. Below in the valley I could see cars streaming down the freeway, but it was with the sound of the city turned off and it lent a sense of detachment to the air. Solitude filled me.

Suddenly the storm was upon us. The intensity of the heat broke as clouds pounded against the mountain, peppering the sandstone with popcorn-sized pellets of water. The smell of the first drops of rain washed over me. Steam rose off the rocks. Rumbling and grumbling in the background were sheets of ear-splitting thunder. And the lightning.

14

For the moment I became frightened, as I remembered that neither mountaintops nor caves were proper places to be when lightning struck, but as quickly as it had pounced on us, the storm dissipated and was gone, and the fear faded with it.

Along the coast, the long curving arch of a rainbow split More Mesa in half. Rays of sun peeked through somber banks of clouds now in full retreat. As the storm faded to the west, the pattern repeated itself. Cloud, thunder, rain.

A half hour later we left the shelter of the cave and made our way to the tawny back of the stone lizard. The sun neared the horizon, and as always, the breeze quieted, leaving an unearthly silence. Colors were trapped along the western horizon—reds, yellows, and oranges that shimmered in the haze. As the sun dipped into the water its shape broke, undulating against the skyline. Slowly it eased itself into the dusk and I was left touched by its momentary grace.

To the east, the mountains gave birth to a second moment of beauty. Moonrise. The globe ascended like a hot air balloon, its light streaming across the valley floor to replace that of the receding sun. City lights were being turned on, but other than that, to the east and to the west, and especially the north, all I saw were the serrated silhouettes of ridge after ridge, like riders on a purple haze.

Stewart Edward White expressed what I felt in his description of topping the Cold Springs Trail at the turn of the century. I have often remembered that description, from his book *The Mountains*, but it seemed no more accurate than right then, as I sat atop Lizard's Mouth after the storm.

It left you breathless, wonder-stricken, awed. You could do nothing but look, and look, and look again, tongue-tied by the impossibility of doing justice to what you felt. And in the far distance, finally, your soul, grown big in a moment, came to rest on the great precipices and pines of the greatest mountains of all, close under the sky.

In a little . . . . the change had come to you, a change definite and enduring, which left your inner processes forever different from what they had been . . . . And often, perhaps a little wistfully . . . . we spoke of how fine it would be to ride down into that land of mystery and enchantment, to penetrate one after the other the canons dimly outlined in the shadows cast by the westering sun . . . . to see for ourselves what lay beyond.

The Playground

In that land of mystery and enchantment is a place where I have spent many an afternoon. It is the Playground, an exposed piece of bedrock a half mile in diameter that appears roughly circular when seen from the Goleta Valley. When I first discovered it, I titled it *Ups 'n Downs* since I couldn't travel more than a few yards in any direction without having to downclimb one rock and scramble up another. But that was before I found *The Narrows* and the maze of tunnels and caves which makes it the perfect place to play hide and seek.

The easy way there is by way of a rough-hewn trail known by the locals as *Lost Hiker*, but on this visit I've made my way down a narrow crease behind a prominent ridge. The ridge which shelters a number of relics from the Pleistocene, including the cinnamon-colored, smooth-barked madrone (which in tree form somewhat resembles the manzanita), the scented laurel, and a number of species of ferns.

Heavy winter snows two years before broke many of the branches in the chaparral canopy, and now the trail is almost indiscernable in the

brush. In many places I crawl to make headway. It is almost, but not quite, the sort of adventure that makes the pain of the stickery bushes endurable.

Finally I reach the edge of the rock outcropping that marks the beginning of the Playground, twist my way through a small opening, up an eight-foot wall, and onto a piece of the rock. Then it is over the other side and down into one of the crevasses which will take me to the very special place I call The Narrows.

There are a number of paths to this hole-in-the-wall, and enough deadends, abrupt edges and the like, to ensure that I will find them all if I come often enough, for it is difficult to follow the same route twice. The surest way (and the brushiest) is to work around the west side of the boulders to the bottom, where they form a prominent cliff. From there the wall seems solid and impregnable, but there is a thin crack that opens to the interior of the Playground.

One of the wonderful things about the Santa Ynez Mountains is its hidden places, such as Teardrop or Cat Canyon, where there are steep water slides and deep pools, or Mist Falls somewhere out in the Gaviota area, or the places of the Chumash rock art—all to be found only by spending many moments of exploration. That is how I have found The Narrows, and as long as I keep this process of discovery alive within me I know I will always have a very personal relationship with the mountain wall.

The Narrows is less than body-width wide, and I am forced to turn sideways as I climb up and over a small ledge and into the interior. A small watercourse moistens the rock and along the bottom is a matting of lime green moss. Through the first part of the narrows I walk with my shoulders touching the walls. It is the perfect place to practice "chimneys" if you are a rock climber, and at one point I place my back against one wall, my feet against the other, and with one palm on either side I begin to inch my way vertically toward the slit of sky above me.

I have to downclimb after I inch my way thirty feet up and traverse forty feet into the narrows, as a bow in the rock sheltering a small bay tree forces me to the ground. Then I scramble another hundred yards to the end of the narrows and into an opening surrounded by headwalls that

force me to continue up canyon. In several more hundreds of yards the walls close in, but this time large boulders and tons of earth have been poured into the opening, making this appear to be a box canyon.

At the base I discover that the rocks have formed a super-structure of sorts and the earth covers it to create a small cave-like entrance leading into a dark interior. Hunched over, I make my way for fifty yards, then it is on all fours to work my way through a tunnel not more than two feet high. There is a starburst of light to lead me on, but at one point the way ahead is in total darkness.

Just when proceeding further seems hopeless the cave makes a dogleg to the left and as I turn the corner I see more light. I can continue on! Fifty more yards brings me to the end of the cave and a chamber the size of a small bedroom. Water falls from directly overhead, a shower of trickles, and the only way out is by climbing a series of boulders stacked one upon the other.

The light is enough to distinguish the interior features, but it is

indirect and soft, heightening the sense of adventure. In one corner there is a teepee-shaped pile of sticks three feet high, the home of the dusky-footed woodrat. The underside of the rock is cold to the touch and the air is crisp, in contrast to the warmth topside. The water seeps drop by drop into a tiny pool, not enough to sustain much life, but enough for a cluster of maidenhair fern which I spy growing by the thimble-sized basin.

It seems a miracle that the space of few feet can separate such disparate plant communities as the chaparral and the ferns, each with such seemingly different needs, plants from climatic periods that existed so many millions of years apart. But that juxtaposition is what makes the vegetation of the mountain wall, nondescript in appearance from the city, so surprising, and so delightful, when confronted up close.

When most people think of the mountain wall, they think chaparral, for it dominates the eye, but pockets of prehistoric beauty still remain, albeit hidden—a surprising beauty that is all the more special because it is rare.

CHAPTER THREE

THE SANDS OF TIME

Man has permanently altered the character of the valley floor along the coast, but the wilderness of the mountain wall, the dense chaparral, and the rugged terrain have defied his rapacity for the most part. It is a land that appears out of place in the modern world of man, seemingly unchanged and unchanging. Its geological structures, however, move at an infinitesimal pace, evident only in the cataclysmic moments when the earth shudders.

The bedrock of these mountains is the sand of time itself, and is always changing, and quite independently of man. The layers of sandstone and shale exposed along the crest of the Santa Ynez Mountains, now thousands of feet above sea level, once lay several thousands of feet below the sea, and may yet lie there again, as the forces of erosion wear away at the resistant rock.

The Transverse Ranges, of which the Santa Ynez Mountains form the most westerly part, is one of the few ranges in the United States that runs in an east-west direction. The Santa Ynez Mountains form a continuous crest, steeply tilted to the south at an angle of nearly 50 degrees, from Point Arguello to Ojai, a distance of 70 miles. From Point Arguello to Gaviota Pass, the range is generally less than 2,000 feet high. East of Gaviota, the mountains gain height rapidly, reaching 4298 feet at Santa Ynez Peak. San Marcos Pass occupies a low saddle formed by a synclinal (V-shaped) fold that crosses the main axis of the range diagonally. To the east of San Marcos Pass, the mountains once again rise, averaging 3,500 feet behind Santa Barbara. The highest point in this part of the Santa Ynez Mountains is near the Santa Barbara-Ventura county line at Divide Peak, 4,690 feet in height.

The geologic history of the Santa Ynez Mountains is related to the slow movements of pieces of the Earth's crust called tectonic plates. At present, Southern California marks the boundary between two of these plates, the North American Plate, which supports most of the continental United States, and the Pacific Plate, which supports a part of the California coast and Baja, California.

The point at which these two plates comes into contact is called the San Andreas Fault. The movement of the plates is called continental drift. The action of this "drift" can cause several things to happen at the point of articulation between two plates. They might be pulled apart, which creates a trench between them. Or one plate can be pushed over the other, a process called subduction. Also, two plates can slide against one another, as presently occurs along the San Andreas Fault. Santa Barbara's geologic history involves all three processes.

The Subduction Begins

One hundred and thirty-five million years ago, the North American and Pacific Plates came into contact with one another for the first time, initiating a series of violent collisions that would shape the geology of all of Southern California. At that time there was a much different topographic relief, dissimilar vegetation (in the areas above water), and a climate much wetter than what we know at present. There were no high mountains in California, perhaps only rolling hills, and a tropical sea lapped against a shoreline much faurther east, near the base of what was to become the Sierra Nevada. The land mass that now is Santa Barbara was underwater and farther south, possibly as far south as northern Baja.

Northern California, however, and most of the Pacific Northwest was above water. Dense rainforests predominated in the Northwest and the climate was warm, temperate, and humid. The climate shifted in southern latitudes to a subtropical savanna, which was the prevailing climate in the parts of Southern California that were above sea level.

The North American and Pacific Plates both began to drift north, but the Pacific Plate moved north at a faster rate. Though the difference in rate of drift was miniscule, an average of only 2 1/4 inches per year (some

300 miles over the entire 135 million year period!), this difference was enough to produce Southern California's rugged topography.

The Pacific Plate was composed, not of a single sheet of the earth's crust, but a series of connected pieces. In its middle portion was a break known as the Pacific Rise, up out of which oozed molten materials from deep within the earth; like escalators, the land on each side moved up and out from the Rise. Thus, as the Pacific Plate drifted north, there was also a part of it that moved to the east, causing the plate at some periods in its geologic history to be pushed, or subducted, under the North American Plate, and at others to slide north against it, as it does today along the San Andreas Fault.

As one of the pieces of the Pacific Plate subducted under the continental piece, the edge of the North American continent acted like a huge bulldozer blade, scraping portions of the crust off the ocean plate. This pile of rubble, called the Franciscan Formation by geologists, eventually would become the basement rock beneath the Santa Ynez Mountains. Today, it is exposed in Santa Barbara County mainly along the south side of the San Rafael Mountains, especially near Figueroa Mountain.

Farther to the interior, the subduction caused widespread volcanic activity in the Sierras, as friction between the two plates caused rock beneath the surface to become molten. It also caused the land directly above the western edge of the North American Plate to sink. As this basin subsided, it formed a large depression something like the shape of a bathtub, and began to fill with sediments. Most of the geologic formations exposed in the Santa Ynez Mountains, including the Juncal, Matilija, Cozy Dell, and Coldwater formations, were deposited in this basin during the Eocene Epoch, 40 to 50 million years ago.

As the basin sank, the ocean moved inland to the base of an ancestral form of the Sierra Nevada, at that time more rolling hills than mountains. As the Sierra range was uplifted, torrential subtropical rains caused widespread erosion. The ocean floor, eventually to become the fertile Central Valley and the Santa Barbara coast, was covered with 20,000 to 30,000 feet of sediment. By the end of the Miocene, about 25 million years ago, the basin had filled and this land re-emerged above sea level.

The sinking of the basin and its sedimentation were not processes that occurred evenly, though. At some points the basin sank rapidly and the ocean was several thousand feet deep. At others, it subsided slowly or not at all, and the basin filled to become a shallow seashore environment. Where it was shallower, a predominance of sands built up, like those which formed prominent peaks such as La Cumbre or the massive pieces of bedrock at Lizard's Mouth. Where the basin was deeper, the shales prevailed, shales like the Cozy Dell, which lies inbetween the Matilija and Coldwater sandstones and forms the deep saddles that make Mission Crags so distinctive.

At the beginning of the Oligocene Epoch, approximately 35 million years ago, the subduction ended, as the section of the Pacific Plate causing it moved north of Southern California. At this point, Santa Barbara still lay beneath the ocean, but as more layers of sandstone and shale piled up in the Channel, in the form of granitic sands and fine mud, the floor rose, and Santa Barbara as a land mass surfaced for the first time.

Perhaps you've noticed the red-colored rocks exposed along the base of the Santa Ynez Mountains. They are especially visible on San Marcos Pass Road several miles above Cathedral Oaks. These are the Sespe "red beds", a series of rock layers composed of shale, sandstone, and a mixture of pebbles and larger cobbles called conglomerate. The reddish color is the result of iron oxides within the shales and sandstones, a vivid celebration of Santa Barbara's rise from its primeval depths. It also leads geologists to conclude that this also was a period of tropical or subtropical climate, since red soils similar to these are being formed in the Tropics today.

At this time California also began to feel the first effects of the San Andreas Fault. As the subducting portion of the Pacific Plate moved north of Santa Barbara, it was replaced with a piece that began to slide against the North American Plate. The two plates did not slide against one another easily. They grabbed at each other, their edges caught. The pressures built, then were relieved suddenly in the form of earthquakes. These forces began to lift the thousands of feet of ocean sediments into the air for the first time.

While the earthquakes raised mountains from the sea, the forces of erosion labored to wear them back down. Streams carried sand and gravel toward the ocean, forming a broad alluvial plain. For 11 million years this gently sloping land received the deposits of sand, silt, and cobbles that would become the Sespe Formation.

THE FORMATIONS

There are eight main rock structures underlying the Santa Ynez Mountains. From oldest to youngest, they are: Juncal Formation, Matilija Sandstone, Cozy Dell Shale, Coldwater Sandstone, Sespe Formation, Vaqueros Sandstone, Rincon Shale, and Monterey Shale. All are sandstone, shale, or interbeds of shale and sandstone. There are some small amounts of conglomerate.

Due the angle at which the rock strata pass over the crest, only the first five of these formations are exposed along the foothill trail system.

JUNCAL

The Juncal Formation is composed of sandstone and shale of the Eocene Age (58 to 36 million years ago) some 4,000 to 5,000 feet thick. The shale predominates and weathers easily. The more rapid erosion of the shale interbeds leaves the sandstones jutting out as prominent ledges or ridges. Near the coast, the layers accumulated in a cold, deep sea which supported little marine life. Due to poor soil quality, Juncal rock supports little but brushy growth on steeper slopes with southern exposures. Near the crest, behind Montecito, the shale has weathered to rolling, rounded hilltops, in contrast to the jagged Matilija formation to the west, and supports a grassland cover. The Juncal Formation is prominent in upper Santa Ynez Valley and is the major rock structure in the Red Rock area.

MATILIJA SANDSTONE

Matilija Sandstone is the rock formation in the proximity of La Cumbre Peak and is 2,000 feet thick at that point. Formed in the later Eocene period, the sandstone is grayish-white, weathers to a buff color and is extremely hard. It is highly resistant to erosion, forming the most rugged, craggy and scenic strata in the Santa Ynez Mountains. Its origin is of granite rock eroded from inland sources. After being washed into the ocean, the granite was decomposed by underwater currents and spread as a uniform blanket of sand over the floor of the Eocene sea as the basin subsided. The Matilija formation also contains no fossils as the cold, inhospitable marine environment continued to prevail.

The upper part of Tunnel Trail passes through the sandstone and Rattlesnake Canyon ends at the formation's base below the walls of Gibraltar Rock. This formation is also found in the narrow, upper part of San Ysidro Trail and just above Montecito Hot Springs.

COZY DELL

Formed in the upper Eocene, it is composed almost entirely of shale. Almost 1,700 feet in thickness, the Cozy Dell Shale readily disintegrates into small fragments and thus forms markedly recessive topography. It is dark gray and weathers to a brownish-gray or olive gray. The shale was deposited as a fine mud, most likely about 35 to 40 million years ago, when the Eocene sea reached its maximum depth. While the Coldwater and Matilija Sandstones on either side form spectacular cliffs, Cozy Dell saddles have their own gentle grace. This shale is exposed in several areas, most notably the connector trail between upper Rattlesnake Canyon and Tunnel Trails, and the saddle between Cathedral and La Cumbre Peaks. The rolling, grassy knolls above San Antonio Creek are also of Cozy Dell Shale.

COLDWATER SANDSTONE

The Coldwater is the thickest of the marine sandstones and forms the pyramid-shaped Mission Crags prominent above the Botanic Garden. Averaging 2,700 feet in thickness, it is mostly gray-white which weathers to a buff color. It contains a 20% composition of siltstone and shale. The granite sands were washed into the late Eocene sea as geologic activities were forcing the ocean waters to retreat. Most likely, the sandstone was deposited as the basin began to fill, giving rise to a marine environment favorable to the development of life. The shallow, brackish seas fostered the growth of large beds of oysters, a characteristic fossil in the upper layers of the Coldwater Sandstone. It is hard, although not quite as resistant as the Matilija strata.

The sandstone forms the picturesque ledges, cliffs and boulder fields of the West Camino Cielo area near the rifle ranges, the magnificent Lizard's Mouth, and the equally impressive "Playground." Most of the rock along upper Jesusita Trail is Coldwater, as are the formations in lower Cold Springs and San Ysidro Canyons. Where it lies near the base of the Santa Ynez Mountains, the sandstone forms a series of narrows, featuring large pools and waterfalls, such as the popular Seven Falls.

SESPE

The Sespe Formation is composed of interbedded shales, sandstones and conglomerates totaling 3,000 feet in thickness. The rock is primarily red or maroon, due to the oxides of iron it contains. It is the only formation of non-marine origin, which accumulated on a nearly level plain as the sea became choked with sediment. The Sespe passes through much of the coast foothills and weathers to form rolling hilltops. Where there is a large percentage of clay in the strata, it weathers to a loamy soil which will support grassy slopes. It is present along lower Jesusita Trail and there are outcroppings throughout the Santa Barbara and Montecito foothills.

NATURAL HISTORY OF THE SANTA YNEZ MOUNTAINS

PERIOD	YEARS BEFORE PRESENT	NOTES
LATE JURASSIC TO EARLY CRETACEOUS	135 million	Continental drift begins 250 million years ago. 135 million years ago: North American Plate begins to override Pacific Plate. Subduction of Pacific Plate causes rise of the Sierra. Along coast and to base of Sierra land subsides to create forearc basin. Sea moves inland to the base of Sierra.
TERIARY Paleocene	60 million	Santa Barbara under deep sea. Climate beyond Sierra to the interior becoming warmer. Sediments deposited on ocean floor as mountains are weathered to relief subducted under North American Plate, and do not appear in strata of the Santa Ynez Range.
Eocene	50 million	Subduction slowing. Pacific Plate being pushed North as well as being subducted. Sediments deposited on ocean floor include basic geological forms of the Santa Ynez Mountains; Juncal, Matilija, Cozy Dell Shale, and Coldwater Sandstone formations. Climate has become subtropical. Large mammals evolve in the lush jungle vegetation. Marine life evolving.
Oligocene	35 million	Pacific Plate has almost passed north of Santa Barbara. Eocene and early Oligocene sediments begin to fill in forearc basin. Sea becomes shallow. The Santa Barbara area rises above sea level for the first time. Purplish-red Sespe formation is first non-marine sediment to be laid down. Climate becoming cooler and drier; vegetation of subtropical environment replaced by savanna and oak woodland. Large mammals become extinct. Several grazing ani-

Miocene	its present position off Washington coast. American and Pacific Plates come into direct contact along San Andreas Fault. Northward-moving Pacific Plate causes shearing stress. Land mass pushed against base of Sierra creates lateral compression giving rise to the Santa Ynez range. Climate cooler and drier; sea life more abundant than at any other time.
30 million	
Pliocene	Santa Barbara completely above sea level and present topography develops. Santa Ynez Crest forced upward, causing depression of Santa Ynez Valley. Climate is warm and dry. Plant communities of the chaparral spreading across Southern California from the Southwest. Many mammals reaching evolutionary peak of development.
13 million	
QUARTERNARY Pleistocene	Uplift of the Santa Ynez Mountains from 1,000 to 2,000 feet higher than at present and further subsidence of interior valley. Onset of series of Ice Ages. Ocean level drops 350 feet, coastline retreats, and the Channel Islands become one long island. Climate becomes cold and moist, and forest plant and animal communities flourish. Crest of mountains slowly eroded to their present relief.
3 million	
Recent	Warming trend develops across continent, and ice sheets melt. Sea level rises quickly. Canyons fill with creek sediments, valleys covered with layers of alluvia and flangomerate. Evergreen plant associations retreat to canyons and mountain crests. Man migrates to area about 10,000 years ago, and has become semi-sedentary by 8,000 years ago.
11,000	

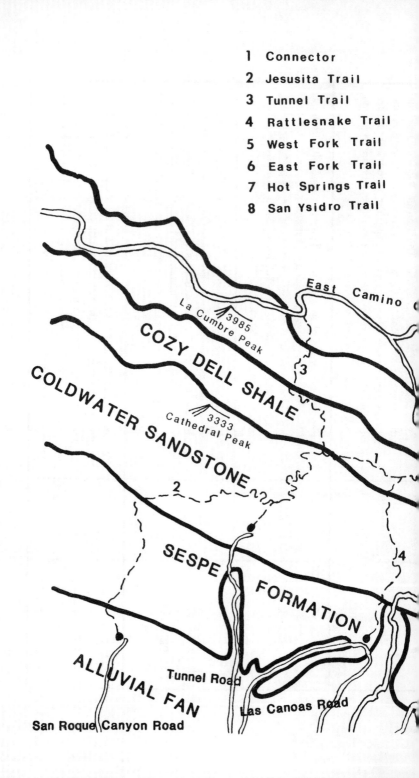

1 Connector
2 Jesusita Trail
3 Tunnel Trail
4 Rattlesnake Trail
5 West Fork Trail
6 East Fork Trail
7 Hot Springs Trail
8 San Ysidro Trail

East Camino

La Cumbre Peak
3985

COZY DELL SHALE

3

COLDWATER SANDSTONE

Cathedral Peak
3333

1

2

SESPE

4

FORMATION

ALLUVIAL FAN
Tunnel Road
Las Canoas Road
San Roque Canyon Road

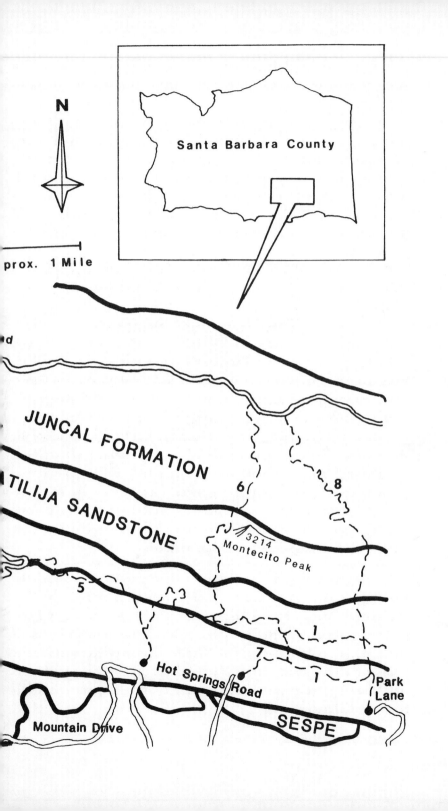

Then the land sank back under the sea, and for another 10 million years the red beds were gradually buried under ocean-bottom sediments laid down in Miocene seas. The warm, shallow seas were more favorable to the development of marine life than at any other time in history. Small, single-celled organisms called diatoms flourished, as did many varieties of shellfish. Sea mammals, including whales, sea otters, seal, and sea lions evolved to maturity during the Miocene Epoch as well. Sediments included Rincon Shale, Vaqueros Sandstone, and the Monterey Formation. The latter two, heavily saturated with organic material due to the abundance of marine life, now play a very important part in Santa Barbara's legacy of oil.

But once again the restless earth shoved these rock layers out of the ocean, this time for good, to form the land we live upon today.

The Changing Climate

At the beginning of the Pliocene Epoch, approximately 13 million years ago, the climate was beginning to shift from subtropical to a drier, cooler environment. Rainfall, a staple of the evergreen forests and tropical plants such as the fern, began to coincide with cold seasonal periods. Cooler ocean temperatures began to affect the positioning of the Pacific High, blocking summer rainfall coming from the Alaskan Gulf and allowing it to occur only during winter and early spring months.

As the cooling, drying trend accelerated, mixed conifer and subalpine forests began to adapt to a narrowing range of environments, and became situated in small pockets and botanical islands of high relief or abundant rainfall where drought stress could be avoided.

By the beginning of the Pliocene, open grasslands replaced the retreating forests, and as the Santa Ynez Mountains formed, they and other coastal ranges became important reservoirs for the survival and persistence of plants derived from the northern temperate rain forests. In addition, the uplifting of the Sierra Nevada began to protect coastal areas from even more intense periods of cooling and drying east of the Sierra, thus allowing the persistence of a number of relic plant species in Southern California.

With the climatic changes, another vegetative community, much more suited to a developing mediterranean environment, spread toward California. During the Eocene, as the layers now forming the basic rock units of the Santa Ynez Mountains were being laid down in the Santa Barbara Channel, live-oak woodland and associated woodland trees such as the madrone, bay, and pinyon pine appeared as far west as the Rocky Mountains. By the Miocene, some twenty to thirty million years later, they had assumed dominance over the interior of much of Southern California.

During the Pliocene, grasslands and an oak-woodland setting covered most of Santa Barbara County, a land of soft rolling hills, luscious clumps of perennial grass, and thick clusters of oak trees—not unlike the Santa Ynez Valley on an April afternoon today. It was not the home of cattle, however, but of prehistoric land mammals such as camels, rhinos, three-toed horses, hedgehogs, and other exotic species that thrived then on the wide expanses of grass.

As the Santa Barbara basin continued to fill with cobblestones, gravels, sand, silt, and other matter, this alluvia formed either rich, deep topsoils or in areas where shale predominated, was compacted to form dense clayey soils. In the areas of good topsoil, grasses became the primary ground cover, with native bunch grasses covering most of the coastal plain. The clay soils, less hospitable, tended to support a combination of grasses and woodland.

Today, in the deep moist soils of the interior valleys of the oak woodland community are the valley oaks, the largest of the American oaks. On the grassy foothills surrounding the valleys are coverings of gnarled little blue oaks, which somehow get enough moisture from the shallow soil to hold their leathery leaves through the dry summers. Equally gnarled, but having greener foliage, are the interior live oaks. They live on stream flats or ravines where the topsoil is deeper and the moisture a bit more abundant. Higher on the slopes, where the grasslands give way to fir and pine, are California black oaks, a deciduous species with leaves similar in appearance to the valley oak but having needle-like points at the ends of the lobes. Along the coast, the California live oak is the prevalent species.

The first oaks to migrate to the west coast were of the temperate forest, primarily deciduous oaks which originated in the cool, wet forests of the northern half of the continent before being driven from the Plains, across the Rockies, and into the West.

But these migrating oaks were a mixture not only of deciduous, but also evergreen varieties. The evergreens, however, such as the California coastal live oak, evolved in a much drier environment, most likely similar to that of the warmer drier parts of northern Mexico, which fostered the evolution of chaparral plant communities.

Perhaps the chaparral plants could be likened to hitchhikers, thumbs out, riding tectonic plates north into a more profitable environment, as movement along the San Andreas Fault caused Southern California to become a mobile zone. The force exerted by this movement generated a power almost impossible to comprehend. It ripped Baja California away from the mainland, creating a trench between it and the Mexican mainland that was to become the Gulf of California. It also broke up the 30,000-foot thickness of sediments that had built up in the Santa Barbara Channel, pushed them more than a mile in the air, and twisted the entire block from its original north-south direction to the east-west orientation it has today. It also moved the Santa Barbara land mass and a host of drought-resistant plants toward an environment whose developing mediterranean climate would allow them to thrive.

Three million years ago, during the Pleistocene Epoch, the Santa Ynez Mountains were uplifted to their greatest relief, perhaps as much as 7,000 in height, as the tectonic pressures being exerted by slippage along the San Andreas Fault caused layers of sedimentary rock in the Santa Barbara area to fold like a wave along the Santa Ynez Fault, on the north side of the range.

At this time a cooling trend also developed throughout the Northern Hemisphere, causing the onset of a series of ice ages. Sheets of ice up to 10,000 feet thick covered much of the continent. The ocean level dropped about 350 feet and the coastline retreated between 5 and 6 miles, exposing the Channel Islands as one long land mass.

For the space of several million years the climate in Southern California was cool and wet. Protected by the Sierras, the west coast endured not ice but torrential rain, which ate away once more at the rising mountains and provided the County with an environment much more like that of Monterey today. It was a period of rich and diverse plant life. Intermixed were conifers, redwoods, and deciduous woodlands. For ferns, such as the maidenhair, it was a period of pre-eminence for them in the Santa Barbara area. The Pleistocene Epoch, like the era of mountain-building, was not one long period but a series of recurring cool-moist, warm-dry cycles in which there was a constant reassortment of the two primary elements: the temperate forests of the north and the drought-resistant communities from the south. Some of the plants sought the high country; others the canyons, or the flanks of the developing mountain wall. Some, like the maidenhair fern, did not seem to mind sharing chaparral country as long as it could receive a share of the meager rainfall.

The overall trend, though, was one of drying, and after the Pleistocene a warmer, less moist climate prevailed, allowing the spread of more drought-resistant plants into Southern California and causing the final elimination of the primeval forests and the ferns from the low country.

With the warming there developed narrower, more specialized local environments. For the first time there was a definite separation into specific plant communities. The drying trend first caused the woodland forests to be segregated into ecological islands where they could continue to exist. Alder, sycamore, and maple migrated to the canyons. Forests of conifer shifted to the mountaintops, while the evergreen oak community was forced onto the thin coastal strip. Other woodland species, which required either a colder climate or more rainfall, such as the cottonwood and valley oak, retreated to more equitable climates in the back country.

Perhaps 10,000 years ago, as the Pleistocene cycles of ice ages and warm, dry periods gave way to the development of a mediterranean climate, the ferns removed themselves to the hidden places like the Playground. For the time being, at least, it was the era of the chaparral. Soon, the first humans would be migrating to the South Coast.

CHAPTER FOUR

THE PATH WALKED SOFTLY

The little Lizard, in order to find out what was going on in the world, would play the flute. And the Coyote, in order to take it in, would cock his ear.

And this is all—the hole of the flute is the pathway to thought.

Kitsepawit

Wind Cave

The spirit of the mountains is not lost. It still remains, lodged in these ancient rocks—a little more hidden now, but there nonetheless and no more so than in those places where the paintings are. This one I call Wind Cave, and in the times I have spent here I have made friends with its ally Night Wind, who blows at times like a soft breath across my path and at others with all the earth's fury.

What it brings with it is a feeling of the circular patterns and on those evenings when Night Wind storms down on me, whipping at my body, hammering at me with its powerful gusts, the mountain seems alive, in alliance with some higher force, a power that I do not as yet understand but of which I am glad to be part.

There are twelve or thirteen other rock art sites in the Santa Ynez Mountains, most in inaccessible canyons or rock outcroppings in the midst of the chaparral, all with meanings equally well hidden. This one is easily available only because West Camino Cielo Road is nearby.

The cave is not large, maybe forty feet in length and twenty feet high. It is more an arching overhang than a cave, but it shelters one of the very

special places of the Santa Ynez Mountains, a place of the ancient people. The rock itself has a mottled appearance, and rows of small cup-like depressions fan across it. Cupules like these were grooved into the sandstone of many of the rock sites utilized by the Chumash as part of fertility ceremonies, and it was believed that they could cure sterility.

I rub my hand across the uneven surface and loose particles of sand fall into my hand. They are slightly damp, a deep earthy yellow loam. The grains, when pressed together, have a procreant look to them and despite the gaunt appearance of the surrounding chaparral, there is a fertile feel to this place.

I sit back against the surface of the cave next to a long thin painting, faint, either a serpent or a lizard. The sandstone wears quickly and parts of the design are no longer visible, the result of the dampness and the inexorable toil of Night Wind.

I am tempted to rub my fingers across the red stain, as if somehow the essence of the painting will be transmitted to my fingertips. I resist the touch, however, as I have been told that the oils from my hand will accelerate the erosion process. Nature proceeds fast enough. I do not need to help.

I want the feel of the Chumash who sat where I am sitting, yucca brush dipped in earth ochres, about to paint private tribal meanings on this wall. I want to perceive the world he saw

Beneath me is a smooth dirt floor, charcoal grey, the result of hundreds of years of evening fires. There is the sense of many eons of moments spent by the Chumash in this place. Countless cycles, sunset and moonrise repeated time and again; ancient harmonies, the power of a universe in which the Chumash were intimately involved. The paintings here represent something intangible, something difficult to draw out of the art work no matter how hard I try.

What sets this apart from other Chumash sites are the steps on the far side of the enclosure, cut deeply into the sandstone bedrock. There are five of them, each six inches high, eighteen wide and a foot deep, the result of many patient hours of carving. They lead to the entrance of a smaller cave.

The opening is less than body length long and two feet high. The inside is slightly larger and is shaped like the interior of an egg. The

paintings are in red—like most of the others at this site—and crude, but they lend an insistence to this spot.

From this perspective, I can see the main part of the cave where a tongue of bedrock, about four feet off the ground, seems to reach out toward the sky. Tucked under it is my favorite painting, its image no longer red ochre but just a rust-colored stain on the coarse sandstone. It is a small circle, six inches in diameter, with what appear to be tiny arms and legs emanating from it, an earth creature whose purpose has been lost in the centuries.

Inside the smaller cave there are several circles, a series of XXX's, a long straight line with V-shaped lines radiating out from it. In the right corner is what might be a lizard design or a waterbug, but the upper part of it is worn away. There are also faint charcoal markings inside the cave.

Chumash paintings such as these belong to one of several distinct style periods which evolved over the past three thousand years. The earliest were primarily charcoal scratchings consisting of narrow lines drawn in black. The second style is the one most commonly found in the Santa Ynez Mountains: red on sandstone. Though simple, the paintings of this period include figures with recognizable heads, bodies and limbs—lizards, snakes, scorpions, centipedes—as well as designs like the ones at this site.

The third style, found more often in the interior mountains, is called polychrome, meaning "many colors". This includes any painting with two or more colors, though the traditional ones used were red and black, and to a lesser extent, white. The polychromes sometimes also utilized a dotted style, with a series of white dots surrounding figures, or dots applied to earlier paintings to make them more elaborate.

Just as the Chumash took food from the earth, they also took the colors for their paints. The favorite color was red, produced from hematite, which ranged in color from dull red to bright vermilion. When found, this mineral is brownish-red, but when exposed to flames, it turns a brighter red. Black was made of manganese oxide, while the white came from finely ground diatomaceous earth, a substance that is composed of the fossils of microscopic algae found in large quantities near Lompoc. Oranges and yellow ochre came from another iron oxide. The less commonly used blue and green paints probably were derived from

serpentine deposits in the San Rafael Mountains. The paints were also traded among tribes; in fact, the finest of the blacks was made by a southern San Joaquin tribe, the Yokuts.

When the wind blows, I think I can almost hear the meaning of this rock art being whispered to me, but as always, just as the breath begins to take on shape and texture, Night Wind sighs again, and the meaning slips by.

The spirit of these caves drifts on, across the face of the mountains, driven by the wind. It is the spirit of the shamans, the ancient ones, who decorated these rocks with the basic elements. It is the memory of the Chumash, people who walked softly through the Santa Ynez Mountains, and the message of their lives drifts with it.

The World of the Chumash

> There is this world in which we live, but there is also the one above us and and one below. Here, where we live, is the center of our world—it is the biggest island. And there are two giant serpents that hold up our world from below. When they are tired they move, and that causes earthquakes.
>
> Maria Solares

Life, to the Chumash, was both mysterious and powerful. Their world offered them an environment more abundant than any other in California, but nevertheless, it set limits. It was a vast land they inhabited—wild, mountainous, and rugged, and topographically oriented in an east-west direction so that the main ranges seemed to align themselves with the movement of the sun and moon.

The Chumash called themselves the *First People*, and most of their villages were situated near the sea where the climate was mild and the food resources plentiful. Over a period of several thousand years, a tribe of people perhaps more prosperous, more artistically inclined, and more highly advanced that any other in California developed on the Santa Barbara coast.

Properly speaking, "Chumash" meant bead maker, which the Indians who lived on Santa Cruz and Santa Rosa Islands were. Subsequently, though, the name has come to refer to all Indians who lived along the coast from Malibu to San Luis Obispo, some 15,000 at the peak of Chumash culture when the Spaniards arrived in the 1770s.

Migratory bands of Indians may have settled in the Santa Barbara area as early as 10,000 years ago, as a warmer, drier climate superceded the Pleistocene ice ages, but it is more likely they arrived closer to 6000 B.C. Before this, most Indian settlements were centered near the lakes and marshes of the San Joaquin and Salinas Valleys and at the edges of the Mojave desert.

As the climate continued to dry, and the wetlands began to retreat, these tribes ranged to the far mountains in search of game, pronghorn antelope, tule elk, and deer. In the Cuyama Valley and the Carrizo Plain, much lusher then than today, there was an abundance of these animals, and progressively the Indians moved west toward the coast.

No historian will be able to record the exact moment the first humans walked onto Santa Barbara soil, but it is known that there were people living here no later than 4000 B.C. These were small bands of people, probably family units, as food-gathering techniques were crude and inefficient and there was a lack of proper storage facilities. These tribes moved often, following shifting seasonal food patterns.

North of the Santa Ynez Mountains, the people focused on gathering food from the valley grasslands, the chaparral, and the marshlands, while the Indians on the coastal strip increasingly utilized the marine resources and developed techniques to harvest the plentiful food supplies there.

By 1500 B.C., the culture that was to become the Chumash nation began to develop in complexity. Villages appeared on the coast as resources allowed the Indians to become more sedentary, marriage exchanges began to occur, and the size of the villages increased—all due mainly to the ability to utilize the ocean more efficiently. The first permanent settlements in the Santa Ynez Valley were also established at this time.

About 1200 B.C.—coinciding with a climatic shift that created a moist, warm environment for several hundred years—the resource base expanded even further and trade relationships developed between the growing number of villages. As the exchange networks grew, shell beads became the standard of value, linking villages on the Channel Islands to coastal villages and in turn to villages in the Santa Ynez Valley and San

Joaquin Valley. Of great significance was the development of the *tomol*, the planked canoe which made the Chumash masters of the Channel.

Prior to this time the mountains of the Santa Barbara Back Country and the interior valleys were used mainly for the collection of seasonal foods—acorns, islay (holly-leaf cherry), or pinyon nuts. The first villages may actually have been seasonal camps for the coastal Chumash. But with the development of basketry, stone cookware, and most important of all, the ability to harvest and store food surpluses in the fall for winter use, permanent villages appeared along the Santa Ynez River and lush streams situated near the base of Figueroa Mountain. As the inland villages prospered, primitive trails over the Santa Ynez and San Rafael Mountains were built.

By 1100 A.D., Chumash culture was relatively complex. There was craft specialization, status differentiation, and villages were run by chieftains known as *wots*. There were also sweat lodges, dance floors, and ceremonial enclosures, and a powerful organization of shaman-priests known as the *'antap*.

The Spirit World

As hunter-gatherers, the Chumash recognized their dependency on the world around them. Ceremonies marked significant times of the year. Fall harvest, for example, when food gathering and storage was at its peak, not only celebrated the abundance of the harvest, but was a period of food sharing and food giving. Winter solstice occasioned several days of feasting and dancing, during which the shamans honored the power of their father, the sun, as he started his journey back toward spring.

Over the span of many generations, the Chumash integrated these ceremonies into a distinctive mythology and developed a very direct and meaningful relationship with the earth. Most of what we know today of this relationship is the work of ethnographer John Peabody Harrington, who interviewed many Chumash descendents in the early 1900s, including Fernando Librado (known also by his Chumash name, *Kitsepawit*) and Maria Solares.

The sky above was *Mishupashup*. There Morning Star, Moon, and Coyote lived. Moon was a quiet lady who lived by herself, while Sky

Coyote was a large creature who watched over human affairs. The world itself was held aloft by an immense eagle, *Slo'w*, who also watched, but was deep in thought and rarely moved other than to stretch his great wings. Morning Star lived in the home of Sun.

Sun, himself, was old and naked. Each day he crossed the sky, carrying a torch to light his way. The torch was made from the bark of a cottonwood-like tree that grew in the heavens. Sun was the fiery giver of life, but it was also well within his power to take it away.

Every night Sky Coyote and Sun acted out the gamble of life in a game known as *Peon*. At the winter solstice, the scores were added. If Sun were the winner, there would be little rain in the following year. If Sky Coyote, who usually had man's best interests in mind, won, Sun had to give Sky Coyote many harvest products to shower down upon the Middle World.

'Itiashup, the Middle World, was like a flat, round island held up by the strength of two giant serpents, and this is where the Chumash lived. The guardian spirit of this world was *Hutash*, the mother earth. Of her, *Kitsepawit* said, "...Earth was the Indian's mother and god, for she gave them their food, and gave the bear, deer and even the snakes and ants their food."

There was also another world, *C'oyinashup*, the lower world beneath the earth. At night, it was said, fearful creatures called *Nunashush* would come from the ground. The worst of these sort of creatures was *Haphap*, a man-like monster whose home was at the foot of a steep peak.

The shaman served as mediator between the realities of daily life and this mystical world. It was a world of power, one in which danger often lurked, a world of chance in which the final outcome was to be determined by his ability to harness this power, which he may have attempted to do through the rock paintings. One of the wonderful things about much of this land, like the Chumash who once lived upon it, is that there is a certain mystery that will always remain to it. There will always be some things about it that we will never know. Like a giant cloak, the chaparral hides much from us, including a great portion of the Chumash rock art, which is secreted in little niches in the high country, powerful visual images blurred just enough to defy interpretation.

CHAPTER FIVE

CANYON COUNTRY

The sharp smell of greasewood, sagebrush and ceanothus is so powerful that it seems almost as hard to penetrate as the chaparral itself. Its richness envelops you, and stains your hair and clothes and memory with fragrance....I have caught a whiff of that aroma and been instantly awash in nostalgia, longing for that spare, glamorless wilderness back of Santa Barbara....this is one of those places whose value lies in depth rather than grandeur. It rewards unhurried attention. Unpretentious, it is a place of fundamentals: rock, water and vegetation. The mixture is utilitarian, rough-hewn, but the charm of the place unfolds to the walker with slow delicacy, like a poppy on a warm spring day. [1]

The rock is hot from the sun and after the plunge in the pool it feels good to lie back and absorb it into my body. The weariness of the hike begins to drain away, and the haste with which we got here seems to evaporate. I look over at Kevin, a longtime friend, and he appears to have melted into the rock. It is a lazy, unpretentious pace we have chosen for ourselves this afternoon, and resting on the coarse sandstone, so many years in the making, it seems foolish to hurry. Instead, we assimilate the sense of deep time which the mountain silently offers us.

Light filters through the oak leaves. The thick trunks of the trees are like dark spires thrust into the the ground by a sky warrior. Beneath, in their shade are smaller shafts with bulbous, bright-red flower pods known as hummingbird sage, and the intense nuclear yellows of the bush poppy. In the springtime these wildflowers create a Mondrian landscape of pastels which soften and give vibrance to the countryside. There are also the honeydew oranges of the sticky monkeyflower, plumes of gold-enrod, long vines of morning glory, and clusters of the odorous pearly everlasting.

A couple passes, more intent on each other than the setting. Then two boys, about twelve, with fishing poles and knapsacks, carefree in their adventurism. The drone of a plane crosses overhead. After it is swallowed by a distant ridgeline, the sound of two jays in the brush emerges—a series of squawks, catcalls, and screeches—in sharp contrast to the sweet sound of the ever-pervading rush of water.

Life in chaparral country begins in the canyons, the corridors into the mountain wall most often visited by Santa Barbarans, thin creases of abundance, a land where wealth is measured in terms not of hard currency but in liquid. Water is the life force here.

I have spent many an afternoon hiking in the canyons of the Santa Ynez Mountains and lying on rocks such as these, and what draws me back is this liquid gold and its cascading sound as gravity pulls it down to the sea. "If there be magic on this planet, it is contained in water," scientist Loren Eisley wrote. "Water....its substance reaches everywhere; it touches the past and prepares the future."

The canyons are places that seem to allow an easier life. The vegetation literally has its feet in the water, and as a result, the leaves are larger and greener than in other plant communities, for these plants can afford to transpire more freely than their chaparral neighbors, which live but a hundred or more feet above.

This community has three distinct layers to it. At the top is the canopy, composed of the long branches of bay, willow, sycamore, and alder, and in the higher parts of the canyons, an occasional bigleaf maple. This overstory provides the shade, coolness, and humidity necessary to the lower layers.

Next are the shrubs, including coffeeberry, elderberry, currant, the ubiquitous poison oak, and the fuchsia-flowered gooseberry, which has brilliant red teardrop-shaped flowers with white inner petals. Also in this middle layer are blackberry, wild rose, and the sunshine brightness of the canyon sunflower.

Beneath is the herbacious layer, including a number of plants which can be classified as fire followers, plants that prosper in the years immediately after fire has swept through an area. Among the herbacious plants are miner's lettuce, hummingbird sage, cream cups, buttercup, lupine, brodiaea, shooting stars, blue-eyed grass, nightshade, water-cress, and mint.

Here the abundance is nowhere more evident than in the numbers of small creatures which inhabit the canyons. To think of wildlife in the mountains one usually thinks of the big creatures: the bear, the lion, the bobcat, or the coyote. But these are creatures more of open country, the grasslands, the wider canyon bottoms, the higher country where the brush is sparser. In the deeper canyons, and especially in the chaparral, the thickets and the interlacings of ceanothus, manzanita, toyon, and scrub oak serve to keep the big life out. The chaparral, as the canyons, are worlds of small dimensions and the little creatures.

The Little Creatures

Though it is late spring, the creek near which Kevin and I lie still runs in volume. Alder leaves accumulate on the surface in places. Some sweep on downstream while others sink as they become waterlogged, and there is a thick layer decaying on the bottom, providing rich nutrients for the small life—the water skaters, the pincher beetles, and the like.

In the canyons of the Santa Ynez Mountains the water falls fast, racing downhill, rarely traveling more than a few hundred yards before pouring into the next pool. The steepness of the mountain wall, an angle of nearly 50 degrees behind the city, and the constrictions of the resistant sand-stone layers causes a pool-drop effect, and inbetween, where the shales prevail, a number of quieter pools exist, which are perfect havens for the insect world.

The hum of the crickets is steady, and like the sound of the ocean, the din does not seem to come from any one direction. Curiously, the sound is more conspicuous when it stops and the canyon becomes intensely quiet by comparison. What kinds of crickets are these? I do not know, but they are part of an ancient tribe. Already old when dinosaurs roamed the earth, they were also the only flying creatures for some 50 million years, before birds evolved as a separate species. They are still the only ones with wings developed as specialized structures (those of all other flying animals are modified legs). It is these wings that make it possible for crickets to create noise, making them the principal instrumentalists of the canyons.

Though they are pitifully small, the water skaters cast monstrous shadows beneath them. But when they propel themselves across the water, they become as graceful as ballet dancers, moving in short spurts with a steady breaststroke. As I look closely, I see that they rest not in the water but on its surface tension, looking to me like miniature trimarans.

Viewed from the perspective of a child, this is an exciting world, and on even closer inspection, face pressed close to the surface of the pool, I see that it is not a sterile place, as I might have guessed had I not looked closer, but is teeming with life.

The skaters have greatly elongated legs and their feet, I learn later, have oil glands which help keep them water-resistant. The surface does not appear strong, yet it must be like a thin, stretched membrane, because I can see that the feet of these bugs make tiny depressions in the film.

While this membrane supports and sustains some insects, it constitutes a barrier to others, which do not have the body weight to plunge through it. Two such creatures, the water boatmen and the backswimmers, I can see making their way back and forth from bottom to surface. Their bodies are coated with water-repelling hairs so that a thin film of air encases each, making them look as if they have been coated with silver. They also have specialized rowing equipment, including elongated hind legs which are covered with hair, making them highly efficient oars. Both look like mini-subs, but while the boatmen swim right-side-up, the backswimmers, as their name implies, move in an upside-down position, which allows them to drift up under their prey.

Other insects, like the dragonfly larvae, are aquatic in their infancy and airborne as adults. The larvae has gills and uses its legs to crawl about or to stalk prey, but if alarmed, it draws water into its rectum and forcibly expels it, creating a unique sort of jet propulsion.

Lying on the pool's bottom, the larvae do not look like the sort of creatures that will metamorphose into the world's most efficient flying machines, but they are as predaceous, perhaps preparing themselves for their future role as top hunters in the insect world. If you look closely on the stalks of poolside vegetation, you will see the shells of those larvae that have made it beyond the water's surface and been transformed into delicate-winged dragonflies.

Home of the Long Legs

Just below where Kevin and I lie, there is a large alder I have climbed many times. It houses a colony of a favorite of mine, the daddy-longlegs. The tree is at least two feet in diameter and is decorated with numerous carvings, monuments to young lovers who have passed by, I suppose. (I wonder whether Rog and Dena are still together, or whether their initials are all that remain of a brief high school fling. And what of Adolph and Laura, who stood under this tree on 8-11-74?)

Today, as almost always, I am unable to resist the urge to clamber up it, to view the canyon world from a different perspective, but mostly to see if the daddy-longlegs are still there. I ascend about thirty feet and find a comfortable crotch in which the letters "KP" had been cut.

The branches are thin, my purchase a bit tenuous, and the breeze that passes through it causes the tree to sway gently, shaking the leaves, but it feels good to be off the ground. From here I can see a tub-shaped pool, a falls, and next to it a small place to sit. No wonder lovers find this an inviting spot.

Alders are wonderful trees. Their bark is smooth, pearl grey, the leaves like green jewels against the azures of the sky. The branches break off easily, I can promise you from experience, but that seems to add something to their looks, a scattering of what appear to be owl's eyes etched into the trunks where there were once limbs.

Directly in front of me, in the pocket of one of these eyes are the daddy-longlegs, their message clear: the more you explore, and the closer you look, the more you see. They lie completely still, bodies huddled together, legs jumbled one over the other, so that I can't tell which legs

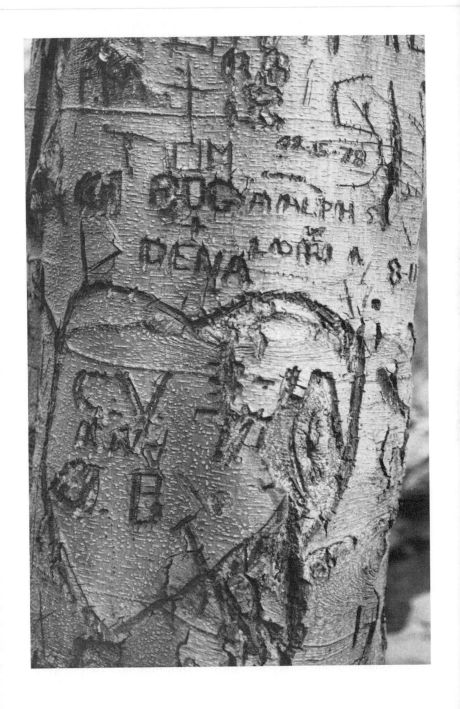

belong to which. One leg waves in the air like a solitary antenna as if taking in surrounding stimuli.

I touch it lightly and it draws back slightly, then returns to its original place. I touch it again, and the second time apparently signals danger, because the mass begin to tumble away from my finger, moving up the tree and over each over like a slinky.

The spiders are always close at hand in the canyon as evidenced by the silk of their webs etched in geometric patterns near our sunbathing spot. I must confess that I do not know my spiders, but I am always fascinated by the sizes and shapes and the colorings of those that inhabit the Santa Ynez Mountains. They are not insects, as many people think, but rather belong to the class Arachnida, making them closer relatives of the scorpion and the tick than of the fly or bee.

In the morning dew, their webs are strikingly beautiful, and though I have often cursed these tiny creatures after catching an invisible web full in the face, I am thankful for their existence—if for no other reason than they eliminate the pesky chaparral flies faster than I can.

Newts and Skinks

Had I not been bitten on the toe by a giant water bug, which probably did not appreciate my presence in its pool, we might have stayed all afternoon. As if a signal to move on, Kevin and I head on up the canyon, to extend our journey a mile or so farther, before turning back. But as often happens, the desire possesses us to see what lies beyond the next corner. Then the next. And the next. In one of the upper pools is another favorite of mine, the water dog, or the Pacific Coast newt, a yellow-orange creature that seems to cling to the bottoms of the pools. Actually this newt is a salamander, but a salamander with a difference, because it has a rough, dry skin which makes it pleasant to handle, as I often did when I was little.

The Pacific Coast newt is an amphibian, a relative of frogs and toads, and one one which demonstrates one of the basic principles of the canyon—that much of the life is adapted both for water and for land. The newt begins life as one of a cluster of about sixteen eggs in a pool. The eggs hatch into tiny babies with gills for breathing underwater, where they remain for over a year. Then they lose the gills and start to breathe by means of lungs. Thereafter they must surface for air every few minutes.

After forsaking its aquatic home, the newt becomes a land dweller, living in damp, woodsy places. In the spring, when the wet season comes, it responds to the rain, returning to its original home to breed. I have seen this occur several times beneath the surface of a quiet pool, male clinging to the back of the female, their coloring so closely matching that of the layers of leaves littering the bottom, that the delicate process often goes unnoticed.

At another place I spy a skink, one of the bright jewels of nature, a slim-bodied lizard which flashes suddenly on the trailside. The skink, a study in water-colored mixtures of beige, black, cream, and flourescent blue, seems to appear out of nowhere, then as suddenly it disappears in a blaze. Its scales are tiny, smooth and very shiny, accenting its colorings, and it is so slick that it looks like it has been dipped in a glossy varnish.

The back of the skink is brown. It is bordered on either side with black and cream lines and its long slim tail is a strikingly brilliant blue. Clearly it is the most beautiful of the chaparral lizards.

The Lure of the Trail

Before we know it, we are far enough beyond our intended destination that we cannot make it back down before dark. Somewhere above us is Montecito Peak, and an upper trail. Should we try for it, though it means a half hour of brush-busting? Or should we stay within the security of the canyon? We are at a fork in the creek where a large, twin-trunked alder rises overhead. We measure the pros and cons of our choices, but in the end there really no choice to be made. Our sense of enthusiasm pushes us on; we have gone too far to stop now.

But which fork? The right one seems to head more directly to Montecito Peak, so we choose it. As we pass the alder, I give it a last glance and on it I see a series of carvings many years old. The first exclaims, "J.P laid Martee here." The second retorts, "B——— S——— ——!" The third, probably the most accurate of all, simply says, "He's only wishing."

We laugh and head up into the chaparral.

CHAPTER SIX

CHAPARRAL COUNTRY

Scrambling up the bank of the right fork, I am already beginning to regret our decision to continue on. This is alluvial soil, built up behind layers of Matilija Sandstone whose narrows have caused it to act as a natural catch basin for sediments. The soil is rich and loamy and it supports a small grove of live oaks. It would be a welcome place to rest if it weren't for the poison oak.

The three-lobed leaves are huge and they glisten, their oily sheen filled with itchy promises. Poison oak lines the canyon sides, and as anyone who has ventured offtrail in any of them can testify, you rarely make it through the dreaded vines untouched. These are especially frustrating—the branches just far enough apart to make me think I can sidestep my way through them, but not far enough to let me actually do it.

Finally we crash through, hoping obliquely to minimize our contact, the oak verdant testimony that beyond here there will be no turning back. Then it is up a dry streambed, scrambling under dead branches and around bushes that have been washed down. For fifteen minutes I become lost in the immediacy of the climb. Even in the shade the sweat pours off me, for though it is cooler here, it is also more humid and I feel more like a damp sponge in this shadowy sauna.

Where Fire Renews Life

We are in the chaparral now and the effort to move forward becomes more challenging, for it is clogged with dead material. The key element in the chaparral life cycle is fire, and nature preadapts this scrubby brush to respond to the slightest spark. It is not uncommon for fuel moistures to drop to 8 to 13 percent during summer drought periods or during Santa Ana conditions. In addition, the close spacing and continuity of the cover and the high surface-to-volume ratios in the chaparral community leads to a high percentage of available fuel.

Over time, the ratio of dead fuel to live plant material increases dramatically. For example, by age 30 often as much as 50 percent of the standing mass of the chaparral is dead, and dry material litters the ground. Where such conditions exist over large mountainous expanses, fires, when ignited, tend to be quite large. Though the chaparral seems tough on the surface, it is actually a very delicately balanced community, well adapted to water stress. Over many millions of years, the chaparral has evolved an equilibrium between water conservation and water use. One of the adaptive features is the solid continuity of the brush cover and its nearly uniform height, which helps minimize evaporation and retain winter moisture through the long summer months of water deprivation. Holding fast to this soil moisture in the summertime is critical, and the even mantle acts like a blanket that protects the soil from wind and solar radiation.

While the cover tends to minimize soil moisture loss, the leaf structure of the chaparral plants is *sclerophyllous*, which means it is well adapted to resist water loss. Some plants, like scrub oak or holly-leaf cherry, have a heavy wax cuticle on the leaves and stems, which helps reduce water loss. On other plants, dense mats of hairs serve the same function. Another adaptation is vertical orientation of leaves, or, as in the case of sugar bush, the leaves are curled so that they do not receive sunlight directly. The greyish color of plants like white or purple sage or yerba santa also reduces the heating up of the plant tissues. Further, sunken stomata on the leaves of these plants help make water loss mimimal. Most of the leaves of the chaparral plants are also *desiccation-tolerant*, which means that the leaf structure resists damage during long dry periods.

Nevertheless there are limits to the length of time these plants can survive water stress and many are *drought deciduous* as well. Often, after 100 days or more of prolonged drought, many begin to lose their leaves, bringing evaporation loss almost to a halt. Plants that drop their leaves commonly develop smaller leaves on side shoots of the main stems, and it is these tiny leaves that enable them to persist through extended drought.

Most chaparral plants produce chemicals that inhibit other plants from invading their territory. Through a process called *allelopathy*, the chemicals invade the soil from the leaf litter and prevent roots of other plants from competing for the soil moisture. These toxins are so potent that in some cases, as with the bush poppy or certain species of ceanothus, the spaces that they occupy may remain open and uninvaded 20 to 40 years after they have been killed off by wildfire.

But the main adaptation of the chaparral to its arid conditions is its response to fire, which initiates a new cycle of plant succession. In the hard chaparral the buildup of dead plant material tends to ensure the continuity of fire, while in the softer chaparral it is the volatile and highly flammable oils that do so.

Afer a fire, annuals and short-lived perennials, called fire followers, temporarily dominate the hillsides, producing spectacular displays of wildflowers. In about two to five years after a fire though, almost all of these species stop growing and their spaces are usually taken by the expanding canopies of the resprouting or regrowing chaparral shrubs. The seeds of these herbaceous fire followers persist in the soil until released by heat from the next wildfire.

Once a shrub occupies the space held by the fire followers, it physically dominates that site, primarily because of its allelopathy. Not until the next fire will the cycle begin anew. Viewed on a linear scale, the chaparral life cycle can be seen as a series of "pulses", each initiated by fire. Removal of the older brush by intense wildfires that occasionally sweep across the mountain wall is not just an adversity that these plants must overcome, but a necessary part of their life cycle.

Unlike some other ecosystems, which require many years to redevelop a healthy diversity once fire has disturbed them, the chaparral is actually healthiest and contains the widest variety of plant and animal species in the years immediately after fire. The concern is not so much if chaparral will recover after fire, or how long it will take, but rather how rapidly the ecosystem will decline if fire is withheld.

Brush Busting

Kevin and I are in the hard chaparral and we see the effect of this fire ecology directly. The branches of the stiff-twigged shrubs make passage within this habitat difficult for us. It has not burned in the past two decades, and except for the outer edges of the bushes most of the limbs are dead. These plants grow only at their tips. Woven through the almost impenetrable tangle are the trails of smaller animals, and though it is quiet and I see nothing, I know they are nearby.

Currently this wildlife is on the decline because as the fuel volume of the chaparral increases, its food productivity decreases. Fire prunes out the dead wood, causes rapid regrowth, and permits the spread of annuals and herbs, which are retarded by the thick overstory. Generally, fire favors wildlife by resetting the botanical time clock back a notch to earlier periods of plant succession and this forces the vegetation to produce more food.

The bed narrows and steepens, a rocky "V" no more than arm's width wide and waist deep. We can no longer stand fully upright, and eventually we are reduced to a crawl as the ceanothus, the chaparral pea, and other thorny plants hem us in. As we move farther away from the main canyon, farther into the wildness of the chaparral, an uncertainty begins to creep into my consciousness. Though it appears that we are nearly halfway to the trail, in actuality we are a long ways from help.

I wonder about the wiseness of our decision to head into the brush alone, and I begin to ask myself the "what if" sorts of questions. Like: What if we come upon a rattlesnake right now? The local variety is known as the Western Pacific rattlesnake, a smaller and less potent version of the diamondback, but venomous nonetheless.

"In the thicker chaparral the rattlesnakes don't always crawl on the ground," a friend named Russ, who owns a ranch in the Refugio area, once told me. "They crawl through the branches." Continually I look back up over my head to see if I am being followed.

There is also the realization that no one knows we are up here. Neither of us has told anyone where we will be going, and if we do not show up at home tonight wonder, who will know where to look for us?

Presently the chaparral seems neither refreshing nor inviting, more prison than paradise. But we are nearing a ridge line, where the going is usually easier, and I begin to feel better. When we reach it, when we crawl—scratched, bruised, with clothes torn—onto the high point, a bitter disappointment awaits us. This is not a ridge that will take us up to the trail, but a cliff. Another fork of the main creek has eaten around behind the one we have chosen to follow, usurping it, cutting it and us off, so to speak, at the pass.

Though Montecito Peak lies in full view, less than half an air mile away, we must descend the cliff, downclimb a steep, overgrown side canyon, and in the darkness make our way up another hillside of chaparral. For even now the light is fading. I am tired. I am hungry. I am thirsty. But most of all I just want to be done. The fun is long past, the adventure has disappeared. It is now no more than a forced march.

Photo by Dick Smith, Courtesy Santa Barbara Museum of Natural History

The descent down the cliff and the side canyon is done faster than safety would normally dictate, but we hurry despite the possible danger. Then it is up the far wall, no longer worrying our way in and out of the brush to minimize the damage done to us by the resistant vegetation. We crawl quickly, pushing, clawing, tearing at the bushes, no longer caring about the consequences.

Two thirds of the way up we stop, on the verge of exhaustion, to rest, to bid the day goodbye, to prepare ourselves for the night. I look over at Kevin. The sparkle is gone from his eyes. His face is smudged with dirt. The sleeve of his T-shirt is torn in several places and he is panting from the effort. Oak leaves and assorted grime sticks to the nape of his sweaty neck, and he looks more the chimney sweep at this moment.

I feel an ant on me and before I can brush it off it bites me, painfully. Nothing seems to be going right. Angry, I crush it between my fingers, and an acrid odor emanates from it, formic acid which renders the ant inedible to most animals. Just then a lemon-yellow banana slug captures my attention as it stretches to bridge the gap between two rocks.

I pick it up and put it in the palm of my hand. After perhaps a minute it pokes a series of eyes out from beneath a lighter yellow, helmet-shaped head. There are four of them, and they emerge slowly, hesitantly, ready to retreat at the slightest peril. The lower of the two pair are smaller, used more as feelers to probe what lies in front of them, and they pop in and out as they encounter my fingers.

It leaves a trail of slime on my hand as it moves, creating a lubricated thoroughfare for itself, and this is what seems most to make the banana slug disagreeable. Surprisingly though, what I most remember about the slug is the feel of the rhythmic contractions that allow it to move across my palm. They are sensuous to the touch.

I place the banana slug on the ground and for several more handfuls of minutes Kevin and I watch its progress. Though its forward movement is painfully slow, the slug glides along, in, under, around, and over pieces of decaying wood, leaves, and stones without the slightest disturbance. In its own way the banana slug is both graceful and delicate.

When I look up, some of the fatigue has gone. It has helped to rest for awhile, to let my breath catch up, but mostly it is this unexpected reward that brightens the moment. It is now sunset, and the canopy is silhouetted black, but through it I can see bits and pieces of orange and yellow on the horizon. Suddenly the chaparral does not seem so confining, our predicament so awful.

In places such as this is the essence of the chaparral. There is no way around it. To know the chaparral you must confront it directly. Caught in its midst, alone, no roads near, the smell of it sunk to my core, I get a whiff of some deeper meaning.

Listening to the sound of nothing as it passes by, feeling the day ebb away, knowing there is an hour, or more, of hardship ahead, I also begin to realize that there is no easy way out of this moment either. But I like it that way. For me it isn't until surrounded by it that the meaning of the chaparral really begins.

Fortunately, from here the way is less difficult. Before long we are on the trail, and we collapse, savoring the firm openness of the path. Lying back, shoulders on the upper slopes of Montecito Peak, with the lights of Santa Barbara in front of us, twinkling in the haze, I could not help but remember the words of Ed Spaulding, whose wonderful book *Camping in Our Mountains* described his boyhood explorations up here:

> Looking back now on these escapades it is hard for me to see what fun there was in them for us. Invariably, after such an exporation, we arrived at our homes scratched and torn and utterly weary; yet there was always the feeling in our breasts that we had done something fine that day and there was always the undiminished enthusiasm for another such adventure.

CHAPTER SEVEN

THE CHAPARRAL BIRDS

It wasn't until I began to spend time wandering off-trail, crawling through the chaparral, or sneaking up undiscovered canyons looking for new experiences that I began to see the wildlife. The amount to be seen often is in direct proportion to the time spent away from the trails, and most definitely in the value placed on the smaller creatures, for this elfin forest harbors the little things. Mostly it requires patience, and the ability to sit for long periods of time, immersed in the chaparral, to let the life come to you.

My favorite are the chaparral birds, somewhat subtle in appearance. As California bird habitats go, the chaparral harbors relatively few species. Though it produces great numbers of plants, there are few plant types, and as a wildlife habitat it is rather uniform and monotonous.

Because of the density of the brush, many of the birds that reside here are specially suited to life within and beneath the chaparral. Near ground level are surface dwellers such as the California thrasher, the Rufous-sided towhee, the brown towhee and the mountain quail, whose running ability enables it to dash through the narrow avenues in the vegetation. It is a pleasure to lie stretched beneath the chaparral and watch these birds scamper about as they forage through the leaf litter for seeds, insects, and other invertebrates.

Living in the canopy itself are the Bewick's wren, orange-crowned warblers and lazuli bunting. When the vegetation is healthy, this layer of the chaparral produces vast quantities of food. Buds, berries, cherries, nuts, seeds, bulbs, corms, and flower leaves are all available. Insects add further to the rich diet afforded these birds, and it is not surprising that, despite the relatively few species, there are large numbers of birds here.

65

Seasons in the chaparral differ from the norm. The primary season for plant growth and flowering occurs between March and May, and this season might be likened to summer elsewhere. June and July can be considered as autumn. The hot, dry months of August, September, and early October, during which no new growth occurs, is essentially winter. Spring really commences with the first rains in November or early December and continues until the rainy season ends in early April, it warms, and the new plant life shoots forth. It is then that the highly vocal but elusive wren-tit seems to sing at its best.

Minstrel of the Chaparral

What is it about the song of the wren-tit, a bird I never see, that so gladdens my heart and opens my soul? I do not know exactly why, but it always seems to pierce deep inside me, and to thrill me like no other sound can.

"Peep peep peep-pee-pee-peepeepepeprrrrr," the well-hidden wren-tit exclaims, a sound that soars over the chaparral. Friends often ask what bird makes the loud, ringing call that comes with surprising suddenness from the nearby bushes, for though they have looked carefully, they cannot spot it. Even if one knows the wren-tit is close by, it is not easy to see this brush dweller, for it rarely leaves the endless expanse of twigs to come into the open at the top or on the ground below.

Only patience will bring them to you, and enough time to arouse the bird's inquisitive nature. With practice they can be glimpsed, but even then it is never easy to see them or to follow them for any distance. I prefer to let this bird remain unobserved and am content just to sit and listen to it sing.

The wren-tit is a curious bird. Individuals probably never go more than a few miles from the place of their birth, and once they have established a nest, they spend most of the remainder of their lives on the half to two-and-a-half acres used during the first nesting. Once mated, a pair of wren-tits remains together as long as both are alive, and they are constant companions.

Together they flit continually through their limited territory searching for food, keeping in touch with each other by frequent calls. The male often pauses to sing, and in turn other males echo back, creating a thrilling series of calls.

The habitat is such that most of the wren-tit's movements are a series of hops or flights of a few feet from one twig to the next. Individuals do not cross open spaces of even 30 or 40 feet either readily or often; a flight of a hundred feet or more is a monumental journey. The wren-tits find their

Photo by Dick Smith, Courtesy Santa Barbara Museum of Natural History

food principally on the bark surfaces of the chaparral plants, and only occasionally will they venture out onto the fruiting stems or surfaces of the leafy plants. Rarely do they descend to the ground. It is after mating that their songs become especially sweet. Ironically, though the wren-tit is not often seen, and seems to prefer anonymity, it may place its nest near a pathside. The nest is usually placed in one of the bushes that make up the wren-tit's territory, most often not in the midst of the denser plants but at its margin where a rock outcrop, lower in height than the bush, or a trail or clearing makes a break. However, they are careful to build the nest in such a way that leafy twigs screen it from view.

The nest, a compact cup, is built by both birds. First comes a cobweb network of material to form a support, then coarse bark fibers are introduced until a saucerlike platform has been created. Then fine strips are laid around the rim to give the nest the shape of a deep cup.

Usually four eggs are laid, all a uniform pale greenish blue, and as the 16-day incubation commences, so does the singing. About 20 minutes after sunrise, the male awakes and begins to sing from his roosting perch. The female responds with her call, and this is repeated often. Then in 10 or 15 minutes the male comes to a branch near the nest. When he is within a few inches, the female leaves, off in search of food.

In another 15 or 20 minutes she returns and the male then leaves. He sings almost at once and frequently while he forages and patrols his territory, and then again when he approaches the nest. Similar exchanges continue throughout the day in shifts that gradually lengthen to 45 or 60 minutes at midday and again shorten toward sunset. Finally, when the female returns near sunset, no more exchanges occur, and the male turns once again to his nesting perch, where he sings his last nighttime song.

There are evenings when I have been hiking down the trail, preoccupied, thoughts pressing down on my mind, and I have heard the wren-tit's call, solitary cries like end songs to the day, and I have been stopped, hushed, hoping for more. The sound has burst forth in quick repetition, a series of whistle-like notes, all on the same pitch, at decreasing intervals until they run together into a trill, "pit—pit— pit—pit—pit-tr-r-r-r-r."

It is the elusive sound of the chaparral, which hides more than it reveals. What it reveals it does so in small bits and pieces, each drawing me a little bit closer to it.

CHAPTER EIGHT

THE MOUNTAIN TRAILS—A HISTORY

> Mountain ranges ever have been obstacles, sometimes an all
> but impassable barrier to man and beast, as they have moved
> about over the surface of the earth; and even the birds in their
> annual migrations have flown up and down the valleys and along
> the coastal plains, whenever possible, rather than face the hard,
> aerial climbs to altitudes sufficiently high to allow them to pass
> over the range crests. [1]

There's just a wisp of a line across the ridge line anymore, a long thread
of a line that suggests more of a past than it does the future. This is the
Arroyo Burro Trail, and it is rich with history. It was passageway for the
Chumash and for countless hunting parties heading into the San Rafael
Mountains. Prospectors used it on the way to quicksilver mines, and later
the Forest Service improved it, as use of the back country increased. Yet
today the Arroyo Burro Trail is off limits to the public, and its future lies
in the courts. The case centers on the ownership of a three-mile section of
the trail which lies on land presently owned by the Rancho San Roque
Corporation.

In 1972, despite hundreds of years of trail use, Rancho San Roque
fenced off the property and posted *No Trespassing* signs at the trailhead. In
1977, the County of Santa Barbara sued the corporation on the grounds of
adverse possession, an old English common law designed to keep property
in constant use. The law states that if an owner has ignored public use of
his land for a period of five years or more it becomes implicitly dedicated
to the users. In 1979, the County hired the Environmental Defense
Center to pursue the case.

The County maintains that the public is entitled to an easement for use of the historic trail because of its "open, notorious, continuous and uninterrupted use" for many years, including that of County Supervisor Bob Kallman, who hiked on the Arroyo Burro Trail in the 1930s as a Boy Scout. A trial to determine the validity of the County's suit will be held soon.

Underlying the suit is something of far greater concern, for sweeping across the mountain wall is a swath of private land holdings, and in these holdings lies much of the future of trail access to the Santa Ynez Mountains.

A short way up Cold Springs Trail, there is a small bronze plaque imbedded in sandstone. It reads:

PRIVATE PROPERTY
Right To Pass By Permission, And
Subject To Control Of Owner
Sect. 1008, California Civil Code

At some point private property crosses almost all of the trails in the front country, and it is clear that if other owners follow the lead of Rancho San Roque, access to the Santa Ynez Mountains could be severely inhibited.

In 1981, Dieter Goetze, chairperson of the County Riding and Hiking Trails Advisory Committee, summarized the situation this way: "In the past 15 years, seven trails in Santa Barbara County have been closed due to private ownership. Another three trails lie within property owned by the City of Santa Barbara Water District. These trails are in jeopardy of being sold to private parties should the public choose to okay such an action. I think that the public good will have been dealt a severe blow if the County loses the Arroyo Burro Trail litigation."[2]

Legacy of the Spanish Land Grants

It is said that the Franciscan friars had a good practical knowledge of the value of land, the benefits arising from a favorable climate, and the methods of cultivating the soil so as to accomplish the greatest results in agriculture. They not only believed in converting the soul to Christianity, but the body as well; hence, they took into account all the peculiarities of climate and soil, which has since made Santa Barbara so famous.[3]

Trail access is a problem with deep historical roots. The problem developed partly because of the pattern of land use the Spanish brought to Santa Barbara, a pattern that tied up much of the front country in large land holdings. By decree of King Carlos III, each presidio was allotted four square leagues (one league equals approximately 4,400 acres), while the Franciscan missionaries were given dominion over the lands under their ecclesiastical jurisdiction, to hold in sacred trust for the Indians.

In 1782 the Santa Barbara Presidio was founded, and four years later the Santa Barbara Mission. Because these two would be in close proximity, they quickly reached an agreement over control of land on the South Coast. These negotiations would have a far-reaching effect on not only on the destiny of Goleta Valley but on access to the mountain wall as well.

According to the agreement, the land to the west of Santa Barbara was to be under the control of the Mission, as well as that to the north, including the Santa Ynez Valley and all land as far up the coast as the Santa Maria River. The coastal strip to the east, including Santa Barbara proper, Montecito, Summerland, and Carpinteria was designated pueblo land under control of the presidio.

With the aid of the Chumash, the Franciscan padres quickly developed an economy near the Mission based on livestock grazing and agriculture. By the latter part of the 1820s, however, the experiment in the conversion of the Chumash from hunter gatherers to agriculturalists was at an end. Just a half century after Portola's expedition, two thirds of these Indians were gone, most victims of disease, and others had fled to the interior. Almost before anyone noticed or cared, the Chumash culture, which had existed on the Santa Barbara coast for longer than the whole of Western civilization, had disappeared.

Revolution in Mexico ended the Spanish experiment in the New World. In 1824, when the few remaining Chumash revolted briefly, as a result of deteriorating conditions, the Mexican government initiated a series of laws freeing the Indians from mission control—albeit too late to do these Indians much good. This was the first step in the dismantling of the mission system.

Feelings against the missions intensified in the late 1820s as Mexican soldiers and citizens at the Presidio clamored for the breakup of the huge land holdings controlled by the Franciscans. In 1833, with the arrival of the first permanent Mexican governor for California, General Jose Figueroa, land patterns changed drastically. In August of 1834, the Governor issued an order secularizing mission lands, a move that had been authorized by the government in Mexico City the previous year.

Figueroa inaugurated an era of land disposal in the County. The Franciscans were relieved of all control of the mission lands. All heads of households and males over twenty were to be given allotments from these lands, not to exceed 400 yards in length and breadth. Most importantly, huge land grants, some forty in all, were handed out between 1834 and 1846 under Figueroa's authority and that of three succeeding governors. Three were issued in Goleta Valley. In 1842, Nicolas Den, an Irish-born physician turned rancher, became grantee of rancho *Los Dos Pueblos*, a

15,534-acre parcel which encompassed most of the Goleta Valley from Fairview Avenue west. A year later the 3,282-acre *Las Positas y La Calera* rancho was obtained by Lieutenant Narciso Fabrigat, the presidio officer who was in charge of troops that followed the Chumash into the southern San Joaquin Valley after their 1824 revolt. The third, the last grant to be issued in Santa Barbara County, was given to Daniel Hill, a Massachusetts sailor who had come to Santa Barbara in 1823, the 4,426-acre *Rancho La Goleta*.

As part of this rancho lifestyle, the 1830s and 1840s were decades of rapid growth in the cattle industry and deterioration of the environment in which the Chumash had lived harmoniously for several thousands of years. Thick forests of live oak were cut for firewood and to expand grazing lands. Native plants were eliminated as the drought-resistant plants of the Southwest prevailed. Wildlife, unable to coexist with the domestic animals, disappeared. Predators such as the grizzly, the coyote, the puma, and the bobcat were eliminated from the valley.

Though the mountain wall remained basically unchanged, the valley, like the Chumash, would never be the same. Daniel Hill, as he walked slowly over the rolling hills of his Rancho La Goleta, saw a land that posterity would never know:

> ...Golden poppies made flame-colored patches on the rounded foothills; between them and the mountain chaparral line, in the mile-wide frost-free belt, wildflowers were blooming in riotous profusion. Lupin, verbena, and Castilian roses made a rainbow-hued blanket on the overflow lands closer to the slough. Daniel Hill, reveling in the clouds of ducks and geese, the herds of antelope and deer glimpsed through the live oaks, was convinced he had stumbled onto the Garden of Eden.[4]

The ranchos continued to expand. After California was admitted to the Union in 1850, the state's population spiralled and trading activity increased. The cattle industry prospered as a result. By the early 1860s, 250,000 head of cattle grazed in the County. Droughts in 1863 and 1864, however, destroyed all but 5,000 of these, and with them the rancho way of life.

Many of the rancho owners, facing bankruptcy, sold portions of their holdings to remain solvent, bringing the first Americans, such as W. W. Hollister, to the area. The future of Santa Barbara now lay with the Americans, who were moving to this rapidly changing area. It was they who would begin to look toward the mountain wall and dream of ways to improve routes across it. Santa Barbara's isolation was about to come to an end.

Early Mountain Trails

In 1804, before the founding of Mission Santa Ynez, the only route through present Santa Barbara County was by way of El Camino Real. This was the same as that taken by Gaspar de Portola on his expedition up the California coast in 1769 and 1770, which followed what is now the route of the Southern Pacific Railroad. Indian trails led over the crest of the Santa Ynez Mountains at the passes, and also by way of Romero Canyon and the Arroyo Burro Trail, but these were not used initially by the Spaniards.

In 1794, Jose Francisco Ortega, the first commandante of the Santa Barbara Presidio, settled on his rancho in Refugio Canyon. After that, no doubt, the Indian trail over Refugio Pass began to be used more frequently. In 1800, Father Estevan Tapis of the Santa Barbara Mission directed improvement of the route over San Marcos Pass, which made it easier to reach Indian villages in the Santa Ynez Valley for purposes of conversion and to obtain sufficient beams to build the houses of Christianized Indians at the mission.

According to the diary of Father Tapis, local Indians volunteered to seek out pines on the distant mountains for the houses, which they found some fourteen leagues from Santa Barbara. The source of these materials most likely was Little Pine Mountain. This improved but still rough-hewn route was soon known as *el arrastradero*, or the haul road, because of the timbers dragged by oxen across its length.

Until the American period a half century later, routes over the mountain wall remained essentially unimproved. In 1860, however, the California Legislature appropriated $15,000 for the construction of the first road through the County, to be cut through Gaviota Pass. Prior to this, Gaviota Pass had been used during the Gold Rush by those on horseback or on foot, but the rocky narrows near the present site of Gaviota Tunnel and numerous stream crossings made it impassable to wagons until the County road was built. Quickly, the Bixby and Flint stagecoaches began to take advantage of the new road.

Then in 1868 a group of Santa Barbara businessmen decided that a shortcut across San Marcos Pass would be lucrative if travelers over it could be required to pay a toll for crossing the Pass. Known as the Santa Ynez Turnpike Road, this route greatly reduced the distance into the Santa Ynez Valley. With the construction of a narrow-gauge railroad from the San Luis Obispo area to Los Olivos in 1886, San Marcos Pass became a busy thoroughfare.

A Civil War veteran, Pat Kinevan, was hired as toll collector. The gate was at the head of San Jose Creek near what is now the junction of West Camino Cielo. The fee charged was $1 for horse and wagon, $2.50 for a stage and team, 25 cents a head for horses and cattle, and a nickel per head of sheep. Soon thereafter, Pat and his wife Nora built a frame house

Photo courtesy Santa Barbara Historical Society

near the toll gate, called the Summit House, which was to serve as the dinner station for the next 25 years.

In the 1870s and 1880s, stage coaches carried thousands of passengers over San Marcos Pass each year. The mountain wall, which had once been considered an almost insurmountable barrier, was increasingly being breached. Many of those who traveled over the crest began to be attracted by the mountain beauty. Some homesteaded, while others later purchased tracts of land near the Pass from the original settlers. As Santa Barbara's tourist industry flourished, retreats such as Johnson Ogram's Painted Cave Resort were established.

The Quicksilver Mines

Use of trails over the Santa Ynez Mountains had also increased in the 1860s and 1870s and new routes were established due to interest in the potential mineral wealth of the back country. In the early 1860s, quicksilver was discovered by miner Jose Moraga on the north side of the Santa Ynez Mountains near the Gibraltar Narrows. There a vein of the precious metal, used to separate gold and silver from the crushed ore, ran in an east-west direction nearly parallel to the river. Two principal claims were established quickly and by the 1870s the Santa Ynez and Los Prietos mines were in full operation.

But access to the mines was not easy. Equipment was hauled over San Marcos Pass and up the Santa Ynez River on a dirt road which crossed the river some 22 times. In October, 1874, the California state *Index of Mines* reported: "Already a graded pack-horse trail has been made from the mine over the Santa Ynez Mountains into Santa Barbara [possibly down Mission Canyon, the site of Tunnel Trail]. By this trail horsemen can go from this city, up and over the mountains, and down to the mines in three hours." In spite of the poor road, the machinery and heavy timbers arrived for the mine construction shortly thereafter.

In March, 1875, a large boiler for the Los Prietos Mine weighing over 4,000 pounds was wagoned over the mountains, requiring six good-sized mules to move it along. The furnace itself was to be built from bricks manufactured on the site, some 140,000 in all. By April there were two main tunnels carved into the bedrock, each more than 100 feet in depth, with as many as 400 men engaged in the mining.

But problems developed. The remoteness of the mines made winter access problematical, and when the river rose during the rainy period, the mines were shut off from the outside world except for the rugged mountain trail. There were also questions as to the boundaries of *Rancho Najalayegua y Los Prietos*, one of the original land grants. Some claimed the grant included the land covering the mining claims; others denied it. Soon thereafter Jose Moraga, who had originally discovered the ore, attempted to jump one of the claims which he thought rightfully was his, further confusing the situation.

Eventually, the mines fell into disuse, despite their early promise. A rapid decrease in the price of the mercury, after numerous discoveries in the northern part of the state, and the inconvenience of the remote location eventually did the quicksilver mines in, but not before the mining efforts had further added to the opening up of the mountain wall.

The Search For Coal

I cannot describe my feelings as I stood on that ridge, that shore of an ancient ocean. How lonely and desolate! Who shall tell how many centuries, how many decades of centuries, have elapsed since these rocks resounded to the roar of breakers, and these animals sported in their foam? I picked up a bone, cemented in the rock with shells. A feeling of awe came over me. Around me rose rugged mountains; no human being was within miles of me to break the silence. And then I felt over-whelmed....[5]

William Brewer

Another form of mineral wealth, coal, reportedly was to be found further up the Santa Ynez watershed, and it, too, involved miner Jose Moraga. In 1862, Moraga, along with several others, laid claim to what supposedly was a rich deposit of this mineral. William Brewer, a member of the California State Geologic Survey authorized by the Legislature in 1860, was dispatched by State Geologist Josiah Whitney to survey this and other potential mineral sites along the coast. Eventually, this continued interest in mining on the Santa Ynez River caused two other trails, the Rattlesnake and Cold Springs, to be pushed over the mountain wall as well.

"Reaching the first peak," Brewer noted, as he crossed the mountain wall on his way to the coal mines, "we struck back over a transverse ridge, down and up, through dense chaparral, in which we toiled for seven hours. This is vastly more fatiguing than merely climbing steep slopes; it tires every muscle in the body...."

"Our lunch was useless, for in our intense thirst we could eat nothing except a little juicy meat," he continued, "Our canteen of water gave out long before we reached the top. I have never before suffered with thirst as I did that day."

But there was also something else that captured Brewer while he toiled through the chaparral, something that would capture others soon. Gradually, as men like Brewer crossed the mountain wall, as stagecoach passengers enjoyed the views while crossing San Marcos Pass or dining at Summit House, as homesteaders began to filter onto the crest, and especially as Santa Barbara became a mecca for tourists, people began to look at the Santa Ynez Mountains as inviting, as alluring, as attractive.

On this trip to the mines Brewer discovered that something else. "The clear sky above, the twinkling stars—to watch them rise over the mountains in the northeast and sink out of sight in the west, to watch the moon rise ... all this is pleasant .... From this summit we had a grand view of the desolate, forbidding wilderness of mountains that surrounded us .... The wild dark canyon, rugged rocks, the dark shadows under the bushes and behind the rocks, the wild scenery on every side, conspired with the hour to produce a most picturesque effect."

At the coal mine he found tools—drill, picks, shovels, and hammers—and signs of intense activity, but the vein itself proved to be a bust. There were a few seams from 1/8 to 3/4 inches thick, a sort of pocket that might furnish a few pecks of coal. "I did not tell the stockholders how very slim the indications were, on my return," he wrote, "but slicked it over by merely telling them that they would not find the coal in profitable quantities."

Interest in the mineral wealth of the back country continued undiminished, however, spurred by the efforts of Moraga and those who backed him. There were further efforts to extract wealth from this land, culminating in the discovery of a pure vein of limestone (now called the Sierra Blanca Formation) along Indian Creek, one of the tributaries of the Santa Ynez River.

The main impedance to these potential riches was thought by many to be lack of access to the interior. Because the route up Mission Canyon had fallen into disrepair after the end of the quicksilver boom, Charles Huse, one of Moraga's partners, pressed the Board of Supervisors to construct another route over the mountains, this up Cold Springs Canyon, which would shorten the distance to the limestone outcropping by about five miles:

> To reach a point seven miles due north of the city of Santa Barbara, it is necessary to go thirty-seven miles by the toll road or more than fifty miles by way of the Gaviota Pass. In the rainy season, as at present, the route up the river Santa Ynez is wholly impractical, by reason of the quick-sands which exist in the bed of the river....All supplies for the mines during the rainy season are sent on the backs of pack-animals over a very circuitous, rough and almost impassable trail over the mountains....If this work is done by the county, the city of Santa Barbara...can be supplied with lime from the interior....In all of the [back country] this county has never spent a single dollar for roads or trails, or for any other object whatever. This region forms at least a quarter part of the territory of the county and merits some attention....[6]

New Trailblazing

In the late 1890s and early 1900s a drastic change occurred when the back country became part of the National Forest system. Concerned by the rapid destruction of forest resources, and, locally, fed by the need to manage the chaparral for water, the public pressured for federal management of what remained of the country's public lands. In 1891, an obscure amendment to an act revising land disposal policies gave the President the power to set aside forest reserves. In 1897, another act, the Forest Management Act, spelled out the terms under which these reserves were to be managed.

One of those was to secure favorable water flows. Faced with an impending water shortage, Santa Barbarans clamored for the mountainous country behind them to be included in the system. As a result, in 1899, the Santa Ynez Forest Reserve was added to the already existing Pine Mountain and Zaca Lake Reserve, and for the first time, the County's mountainous territories were under the direct management of the federal government.

The first trail created during this new era was the La Cumbre Trail, one you won't find listed anymore. It has been fifty years since anyone has used this path, because it was subsequently widened and paved to become Gibraltar Road.

On New Year's Day in 1902 the *Santa Barbara Morning Press* speculated: "Someday there will be an easy wagon road leading up to La Cumbre, to accommodate vehicles and the automobile; and it is quite within the range of possibilities that a trolley-line may be constructed to the place, getting its power from the Mission falls, and which will course the summit of the range and add one more to the great wonders of the world."[7]

A trail construction committee composed of members of the Chamber of Commerce began a campaign early in 1902 to raise funds, estimated at that time to be some $400 to $500. At the same time they proposed to rework the overgrown and rundown Rattlesnake Canyon Trail, which had been constructed earlier in part by Jose Moraga and by a man named Flores, who owned a homestead at the head of the canyon.

Work was carried out primarily by rangers in the newly created Forest Service. Beginning in Sycamore Canyon, the La Cumbre trail intersected the present location of Gibraltar Road about a mile up from Mountain Drive at a large promontory, the original Inspiration Point. As the trail was ascended, one encountered various views, all named by the Chamber of Commerce. These names emphasized the new attitude Santa Barbarans had about the mountains behind them.

The first view of Montecito was called *El Contento*, or the place of contentment; the first glimpse of Goleta Valley was *El Reposo*, or tranquility. At the 1,700 foot elevation was *La Roca Grande* (the great boulder); a spot at 2,400 feet was called *El Encanto*, meaning the enchanting place.

At 2,900 feet a large block of sandstone, known today as Gibraltar Rock, was entitled *Centinela del Abismo*, or the sentinel of the abyss. Just beyond was Flores Flat or *El Descanso*, the resting spot. At the 3,300-foot summit, one found *La Sorpresa* or the surprise, where one could see the San Rafael Mountains for the first time.

This increased use of the mountains was due primarily to the tourist boom, itself made possible by the transportation revolution, begun by the construction of the Gaviota Road. In 1887, when the Southern Pacific Railroad completed a branch line from Los Angeles to Santa Barbara, even more people began to travel to the area. Then in 1892, after Lillard and Catlett, the owners of the property traversed by the stage coaches, closed the old stage road, a newer, more practical route over San Marcos Pass was built, making it much easier to travel into the Santa Ynez Mountains. A decade later, the age of the automobile came to Santa Barbara via this new road, when a Locomobile steamer piloted by George Beauhoff of Philadelphia chugged over the summit on March 28, 1901.

Three days later the last stage coach traversed the Pass, for on that day the Southern Pacific Railroad completed its connection between Los Angeles and San Francisco, and in the process it ended Santa Barbara's isolation forever.

Trail Use Declines

During the first decade of the century, other trails were built as the result of the increased number of people coming to Santa Barbara. The San Ysidro Guest Ranch pushed a horse trail to the summit, and as hunting and fishing became more popular, the Franklin and Rincon trails were built in behind Carpinteria to give better access to the upper Santa Ynez drainage.

The Forest Service also contributed to the popularization of the back country, as the forest rangers improved and extended the trails over the crest. In 1910, with the support of a $10 million federal appropriation for the improvement of roads within the forest reserves, the local mountains became much more accessible by auto. First a rough road was cut from San Marcos Pass Road to Los Prietos, following substantially the same route used by the quicksilver miners. At the same time the County began to improve the roads over the passes, spurred by such men as wealthy Santa Barbaran George Owen Knapp, who had purchased from Homer Snyder one of the original homesteads on the crest.

Unfortunately, these efforts to develop access to the mountains eventually eliminated use of many of the front country trails that were so popular at the turn of the century. Ironically, despite the larger number of people who hike in the Santa Ynez Mountains today, there are fewer trails open now than there were then.

In the 1930s, with the aid of thousands of Civilian Conservation Corps workers, the early roads were further improved, others were added, and as this occurred, use of the front country trails diminished. There was no longer the need to ride by horseback over the crest, for it was now easier to trailer one's horse over the Pass to Upper Oso or Pendola than to ride over the crest. By the late 1930s, most hunters no longer used the foothill trails, nor did the tourists, once the automobile gave them increased mobility.

The Forest Service contributed to this diminished use in another way: in 1934, the *Gibraltar Closed Area* was put into effect in the Santa Ynez watershed, restricting travel there during fire season. Then, during World War II, the back country was closed entirely because there wasn't sufficient personnel to supervise regulated use.

By the 1950s many of the historic front-country trails had fallen into almost complete disuse. Among them were the Arroyo Burro, Franklin, and Romero Canyon trails. Concurrently, much of the private land, held in large blocks since the era of the land grant, was being broken up into smaller parcels. As the foothill property was subdivided and used for speculative purposes, ownership changed somewhat frequently.

As the land passed through a series of hands, owners became accustomed to the lack of trail use. In fact, many of the owners were not even aware that historic trails passed through their property. And once the trails were closed, few of the owners wanted hikers to begin crossing their land again. Some were avocado growers, such as the owners of Rancho San Roque, who feared that a fungus known as cinnamon root rot would be brought onto their property on hikers' shoes.

Others had purchased property away from the city to live in the peace and quiet the foothills offered and didn't want scores of hikers invading their solitude. There were those, too, like the owner of the land above the San Antonio Creek Trail, whose land value would fall as much as $600,000, according to appraisals, should a trail cut through the middle of the property.

The Future

Today, trails in the Santa Ynez Mountains are as popular as ever, and despite the legal problems affecting some of them, they offer something special that few other locales besides Santa Barbara have to offer. They are there to appreciate, and to enjoy. They are both beautiful and fragile, and they need the care of all of us.

In them is the history of this land, the geology, the chaparral plant community, and the hidden vegetation. Also there is the heritage of the Chumash, and of pioneer miners and homesteaders. There are many messages these mountains have to offer. Please take care of them.

CHAPTER NINE

THE HIKES

Even though the foothill trails aren't long and you are never far from help, it is a good idea to bring along a few items. A map is beneficial since there are few trail markers and many "informal" side paths. A good general map can be obtained from the Los Padres National Forest headquarters at 42 Aero Camino, Goleta for $1.00. For more detailed information you can purchase a topographical (topo) map for the area in which you want to hike. These maps are invaluable aids and are also available for approximately $2.00 at the Forest Service or at Upper Limits and Granite Mountaineering backpacking stores in Santa Barbara.

The Santa Ynez Mountains run east-west, so orienting yourself here may prove more difficult than it is elsewhere along the California coast. When looking inland toward the mountains you face north rather than east. Thus, when hiking up most of the canyons behind Santa Barbara place your topo with the north, or upper, edge facing upcanyon.

It is also wise to bring a small first-aid kit with you as minor injuries are always a possibility. Rattlesnake sightings are infrequent, but they do live in these mountains, so take care where you step and where you place your hands. You might consider carrying a snakebite kit, but unless you know how to use it properly, it is probably safer to hike out for help.

While water would seem to be unnecessary on hikes along stream systems, do bring along a supply—one or two quarts per person—as a precaution. During summer and fall some of the creeks are either dry or run so slowly as to become either contaminated or stagnant. Also be wary of drinking water where there are signs of horseback riding! Be sure to carry extra water if you are planning on hiking out of the canyons, as most of the trails up the mountain wall are hot and dry.

Additional information on the trails, the geology, and the plant and animal life may be obtained at the Santa Barbara Botanic Garden or the Museum of Natural History. Also the Los Padres Interpretive Association has a number of books and maps available at the Forest Service headquarters.

If there is an accident help can be obtained easily. Have one of the party members hike out to a telephone and call the Sheriffs Department (967-5561). They can activate the Los Padres Search and Rescue Team if needed.

Happy hiking!

SAN ANTONIO CREEK TRAIL

Tuckers Grove (148′) to intersection with San Marcos Pass
   Road
TOPO: Goleta (trail not marked on map)
DISTANCE: One and one-half miles
ELEVATION GAIN: +352 feet
GRADE: Easy

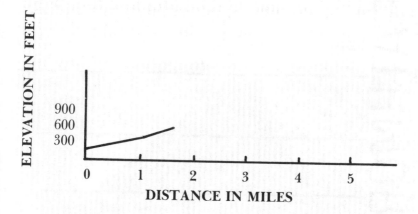

The San Antonio Creek Trail begins at Tucker's Grove. In the late 1800s this sheltered oak grove served as a favorite picnic area for Santa Barbara's Scottish-American population. It was privately owned by Charlie Tucker, a popular valley resident who maintained the sylvan retreat for public use free of charge until he died in 1912. Shortly thereafter it was purchased by rancher George S. Edwards who deeded it to the county, thus allowing it to become one of the valley's first public parks.

★ ★ ★

The trailhead is near the rear of the Grove. Drive through the park and into the paved parking area. Continue through it and across San Antonio Creek to a second parking area. You can pick up the trail there near a small sign that says "Bridle Path", although most hikers continue to the end of the lot where Kiwanis Meadows begins because this eliminates a

stream crossing. Follow the wooden fence on the creek side of the meadows to an opening onto the trail.

The San Antonio Creek Trail is one of the most pleasant of the short hikes, especially for those of you who want to take younger children along with you. In the spring, with the cascading waters of the creek flowing cool and clear, the oak woodland and canyon vegetation provide just the touch of color, richness, and variety for an hour or two of relaxed hiking.

Though the trail is unmarked, the well-used path is relatively easy to follow. It meanders first for a half mile on the east side of the creek through a large oak meadow. Just past Kiwanis Meadow the canyon begins, and the hillside, covered with ferns and sorrel, is shaded by numerous oaks. There is poison oak along here as well, so take care, especially with children.

The oak meadow has numerous trails radiating through it, perfect for children to play on, and the air has the sweet smell of bay and California sage. In the early morning, light filtering through the trees gives this grove a cathedral-like atmosphere.

From here the trail opens for a while, then closes back in. In places the path is not much more than a shoulder-width wide and is rutted a foot deep in the sandy soil. The tunnel-like enclosure hems one in with the aroma of the soft chaparral. Nearby are the sounds of the hidden creek and numerous birds.

The trail reaches an opening once more, this one filled primarily with sycamore, and the trail makes several lazy "S" curves and crosses the creek. Out of sight along here is a farm, but a meadow dotted with Christmas-tree pines is evidence that it is not too far away. Immediately cross the creek once more and hike up onto a bench, which leads to a large flood-control dam.

There the trail crosses the dam and turns upstream. While several trails appear to be leading upstream from this point, the main path turns right and crosses the creek and passes by a long chain-link fence, which you can see before you make the crossing. The other trails lead up onto San Antonio Creek Road to provide horse riders access to the canyon. One of these continues along the west bank, though the trail on this side is fairly overgrown.

On the east side the trail wanders through a most enjoyable section, thick with oaks, thistle, and blackberry interspersed between large cream-colored boulders. In a half mile the trail intersects with Highway 154, where the trail ends under the bridge, near the beginning of the Vista Del Mundo Ranch.

In the future the San Antonio Creek Trail will continue on to intersect with the Arroyo Burro Trail and thence to the crest, where it will feed into recreational areas in the upper Santa Ynez drainage. Inbetween the trail's present ending point and the National Forest boundary lies a large block of private property which has hindered efforts to extend it into the forest. In the spring of 1975 the California legislature passed Senate Bill 301 authored by Senator Omer Rains (co-authored by Assemblyman Gary Hart of Santa Barbara), which provided for the expenditure of nearly $1 million for the purpose of expanding the state riding, hiking, and bicycling trails system in Santa Barbara and Ventura counties. The aim was to create a series of links for non-motorized travel between the state park system, National Forest trails, and major urban areas.

In Santa Barbara, this included provisions for paved bike trails along Atascadero and Maria Ygnacio creeks, which have since been constructed (including the bike path to Goleta Beach). Eventually these trails will connect to El Capitan, Refugio, and Gaviota state parks, and also the San Antonio Creek Trail when negotiations have been completed with the property owner above Highway 154.

JESUSITA TRAIL

Stevens Park or Cater Water Filtration Plant (358′) to
 Tunnel Trail (1000′)
TOPO: Santa Barbara
DISTANCE: Four and one-half miles
ELEVATION GAIN: +642 feet (high point is 1500′)
GRADE: Easy to Moderate

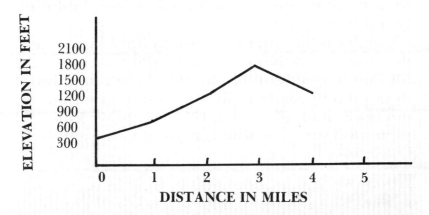

Jesusita Trail is unlike the other foothill trails, which begin in the lower canyons and then extend upward through the chaparral to East Camino Cielo or Gibraltar Road. Rather, it is a loop, connecting San Roque and Mission Canyons via Inspiration Point and its awe-inspiring panoramas.

The Jesusita is not one of the historic trails but was built in 1964 as part of an $8,000 project financed by the State Division of Beaches and Parks after an exchange of easements between the County and the Marion Moreno family, who owned most of the upper canyon.

You can begin the trail either at Stevens Park, just below San Roque Bridge on Foothill Road, or just past Cater Filtration Plant on San Roque Road. For those who would like to start at the park, perhaps for a picnic or midday game of volleyball beforehand, drive up San Roque Road (Las

93

Positas exit off Highway 101) from State street to Calle Fresno. Turn left and follow it for a quarter mile to the park entrance.

Jesusita Trail might be divided into two sections. The first, about a mile and a half long, wanders back and forth through coastal sage and small oak meadows. San Roque Creek, filled with sediment, supports many plants that thrive on disturbed environments, such as anise, castor bean, mustard, and poison hemlock. The elevation gain is gradual and the trail, though a bit difficult to follow at times, provides access to lush canyon vegetation, quiet pools, and a welcome solitude. Children will find it a delight.

From the park hike along the east side of the creek for a quarter mile, then cross to the west side and look for the trail as it passes over a small hill. From the top of the hill you will see a flood-control dam. Following the left side of the basin behind the dam for several hundred yards then crossing and hiking up a short steep hill will bring you to Jesusita Trail proper, which intersects from the right. Just up the trail from there is Cater Filtration Plant.

Turn left and head back down into the canyon. From there the path lazily crosses back and forth through oak meadows, clusters of small shrubs, and, numerous times through the creek. There are several side paths along the way, which lead to pools or rock outcroppings, but the way shouldn't be too confusing as the main trail is rather well worn. In a half mile the trail turns right, heads up onto a long plateau covered with annual grasses then retreats back into the canyon. On the west side of the creek is a private dirt road which is not part of the trail. Please keep to the trail. Another quarter mile brings you to Moreno Ranch, marked by a horse corral, and the end of the lower section of the trail.

The upper chaparral section begins here and leads to Inspiration Point. Also, the creek branches at this point. The West Fork has a dirt road leading up it, which is closed off by a locked gate. This goes to Rancho San Roque. Nearby is the trailhead to the Arroyo Burro Trail which is currently not open to the public.

Jesusita Trail turns to the northeast and eventually winds up the East Fork. There are signs leading to this section, which will help you avoid private holdings here. The owners would be extremely grateful if you would stay to the trail rather than meander onto their property.

Several hundred yards up the East Fork the trail passes through a thin but spectacular layer of Vaqueros Sandstone, then rises sharply via a series of switchbacks up into the chaparral. This area is dominated by chamise, ceanothus, holly-leaf cherry, and manzanita. The trail levels somewhat at this point, turns east, and continues along the Sespe redbeds before widening to become a power line road, which marks the beginning of Coldwater Sandstone. Towering overhead are the precipitous Mission Crags. The toothlike shape of Cathedral Peak can be seen a thousand feet above.

At the base of the 300-foot-tall spire is an enormous cave which, according to legend, harbored stolen horses during the early 1800s. It is seldom visited except during the few years after a wildfire, as *News Press* writer Dick Smith did in 1966, two years after the Coyote Fire. "The view from Cathedral Peak is truly sensational, much closer and equally as high as that from La Cumbre Peak," he noted. "One can look down on the entire city, unobstructed by any foreground ridge." However, he continued, "Getting to take a look at this fabulous view is not an easy task. In fact it took…nearly two hours of rock hopping to gain the end of the ridge….There's no trail. You must pick your way across the brush."

In another few hundred yards is Inspiration Point, though it is actually not at the high point but rather at the east end of the knoll where the power line road ends. A small trail leads to a series of boulders that marks the view point. You'll know you are there if you spy the initials carved a half century ago in the bedrock.

From Inspiration Point Jesusita Trail continues another three-fourths mile, winding down into the west fork of Mission Creek. Nearby is the fabled Seven Falls. For hundreds of thousands of years the forces of erosion have eaten away at the Matilija Sandstone which forms the bulk of La Cumbre Peak, and the grinding power of the sand and water as they tumbled downhill has etched magical shapes in the rock formations below. One of these is a series of small falls and deep potholes that lie one after the other.

"A pleasant party spent yesterday up Mission Canyon, visiting the noted Seven Falls and afterwards eating a tempting picnic dinner in a romantic spot on the creek's banks. To reach these falls requires some

active climbing, able bodied sliding and skillful swinging...." A recent quote? Not so, for this paragraph came from the *Santa Barbara Daily Press* in 1876, a reminder that this hidden spot has long been used as a getaway.

You can return to your starting point by retracing your steps back along Jesusita Trail or you might consider bringing another car along and parking it beforehand at the Tunnel Road trailhead to use as a shuttle. If so, also consider carrying a flashlight so you can stay for sunset at the Point before heading down.

TUNNEL TRAIL

**End of Tunnel Road (1000') to intersection with East Camino
  Cielo (3350')**
TOPO: Santa Barbara
DISTANCE: Four miles
ELEVATION GAIN: +2350 feet
GRADE: Steep

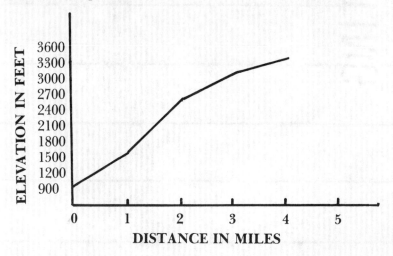

Tunnel Trail received its name just after the turn of the century. Though Santa Barbara had a population of only 6,500 then, the city was already in the midst of its first water shortage, brought on partly because of the increased numbers of people coming to the area after the Southern Pacific Railroad completed a branch line here from Los Angeles in 1887. Droughts in the late 1890s also contributed to the problem.

In 1903 J.B. Lippincott, engineer for the U.S. Geological Survey, proposed that the city construct a tunnel through the Santa Ynez Mountains to connect to the Santa Ynez watershed on the north. The project was begun in 1904 and completed in 1912. Workers on both sides burrowed deep into the mountain flanks for eight long years, encountering many obstacles before they finished.

The tunneling began from the south portal on April 29, 1904. After the excavation crew had progressed 1700 feet into the mountain, they encountered quicksand. Sulphur water was the next obstacle and it was heavily charged with hydrogen gas which affected the eyes of the workers, who were forced to work in one-hour shifts. Then these and other gases caused a fungus to attack the supporting timbers, destroying them and forcing the use of concrete to shore up the walls.

On the north side, pockets of marsh gas were found from time to time and safety lanterns were carried by workers as the gas would ignite otherwise. According to Lee Hyde, whose father was chosen by Lippincott to engineer the project, "On one occasion, two brave men, while literally taking their lives in their hands, went into the tunnel, ignited the gas by torch, then lay prone beneath the body of the flame. The heat was, of course, terrific and the men survived by turning over and over in the water that was flowing below."

A small electric train was used to carry the men into the tunnel and the excavated material out. In 1912 another potential disaster was averted when a cave-in was discovered. The train operator then reversed his direction and picked up eight men who were farther on in the tunnel. At the point where they encountered the cave-in the men were forced to wade armpit-deep through the mucky water to escape out of the tunnel. Though the men were saved, it was necessary to detour around the spot and wait a year for it to dry out enough that the tunnel could be straightened at that point.

From 1912 until Gibraltar Dam was completed in 1921, supplies went through the tunnel on the miniature electric train. In addition, a trail that had originally been constructed to the quicksilver mines near the site of the dam was recut, and eventually became known as Tunnel Trail.

★ ★ ★

The trailhead begins at the end of Tunnel Road. Drive up Mission Canyon Road to the Tunnel Road turnoff, a half mile before the Botanic Garden, and continue several miles to the end. Park in the proper spaces there, for police frequently ticket illegally parked cars. The trail begins about three quarters of a mile beyond the locked gate.

Walk up the paved road, which continues steadily uphill, until a hundred yards before Mission Tunnel, where the road turns sharply to the left and then curves past the West Fork of Mission Creek and a small building. Below it is the tunnel. At the high point before heading down to the tunnel, look for a stairway, which leads down into the main canyon and to a beautiful pool known as Fern Falls.

Past Mission Tunnel is the trailhead. Fifty yards after the paved road ends, marked by a California Riding and Hiking trail sign, Tunnel Trail begins. The steep winding path passes through the four geologic formations of the Eocene epoch on its three-and-a-half mile length. At the trailhead Coldwater Sandstone predominates. Both the east and west forks of Mission Creek have eroded through the highly resistant sandstone in spectacular fashion, forming in the upper off-trail sections a series of narrows with deep pools, steep falls, and rich green fern coverings.

Above, the trail begins a series of switchbacks out of the sandstone and up a ridgeline between the two forks. After about three quarters of a mile the path turns left and around a large knoll that marks the end of this formation. Just beyond, in a large saddle formed by the weathered Cozy Dell Shale, is a connector trail winding down to Rattlesnake Canyon. From there the main trail continues northwest for several miles up to Camino Cielo.

Approximately a half mile beyond the connector trail you will pass through the rugged and highly scenic crags of Matilija Sandstone. Another one third to one half mile farther along a small creek crosses the trail. Below the trail, but hidden from view by the chaparral cover, is a sandstone bench on the upper edge of the 200-foot-high Mission Falls. In springtime, with the creek flowing at its maximum, the spot is an ideal sunbathing and picnicking area. The view is breathtaking. It is also a wonderful place to view the sunset, but if you stay late be sure to bring a flashlight along for the trip back to the car.

After crossing the creek, the trail wanders for a half mile through the sandstone. Then, as the canyon narrows, you enter the Juncal Formation. After this, the trail then meanders back and forth around small rounded knolls formed by the easily weathered shale to a saddle at East Camino Cielo known as Angostura Pass. La Cumbre Peak is an additional three quarters of a mile to the west on the paved road.

You can also continue down the dirt road on the north side of Angostura Pass, which ends in six miles at Gibraltar Dam. About two miles down the road a trail leads to the west to Matias Potrero.

RATTLESNAKE CANYON TRAIL

Skofield Park (900′) to intersection with Gilbraltar Road (2450′)
TOPO: Santa Barbara
DISTANCE: Three miles
ELEVATION GAIN: +1550 feet
GRADE: Moderate

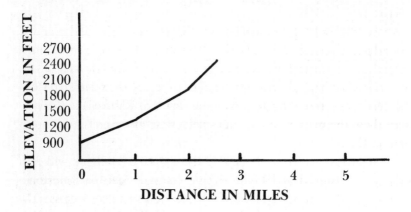

Rattlesnake Canyon has seen constant activity since early Mission days. In the 1790s, water was supplied to the Mission and the Presidio through a ditch from Mission Creek. Chumash helped dig it and they constructed a temporary dam of brush, earth, and rocks. Eventually, in the years 1790 to 1795, artisans were sent from Mexico to assist in the building of houses and more permanent water storage facilities.

Initially a large stone dam and an aqueduct were built in Mission Creek and in 1808 another dam was added in Rattlesnake Canyon. With Indian labor the fieldstone and mortar structure was built across the creek about a half mile up from Las Canoas Road. While remnants of the dam still exist, sediments have filled in behind, eliminating the reservoir and carving a V-shaped notch in the middle of the dam. However, the pool below, shaded by alder and bay, and surrounded by wood ferns and the colorful tiger lily still provides welcome relief from the hot afternoon sun.

The trail begins just before the entrance to Skofield Park, near a delicately shaped stone bridge. Drive up Mission Canyon past Tunnel Road to Las Canoas. Turn right and continue a mile and a half to an open area immediately preceding the bridge. There you'll find a large sign denoting the start of Rattlesnake Canyon Trail.

From there, cross the creek and follow a short connector trail to a wider dirt road. For many decades this was a buggy road which ran alongside the creek to a point about three quarters of a mile upstream where a prominent layer of sandstone crossed the creek. This was the location of a stone quarry from which much of the stonework in Montecito was derived.

The old buggy road rises gradually through rolling sage-covered hills and the Sespe Formation, then heads back to the creek and the first of a series of narrows created as the stream eroded through successive layers of Coldwater Sandstone during the Pleistocene mountain-building process.

Numerous side trails lead off the main path through the sages to small oak meadows, and they provide access to waterfalls as well as to the old Mission Dam. Beware the poison oak, though!

After the narrows, the trail crosses the creek and follows a set of switchbacks up a steep hill which opens to a large grass meadow marked by a series of scattered pines. In the early 1930s the original trees were planted by Hobart Skofield whose wealthy father, attracted by its beauty and serenity, had purchased most of the land in the canyon.

Placing rawhide baskets on either side of his palomino horse, Hobart packed the young trees in them and started up to the meadow. But apparently the horse bucked part way up the trail when it caught sight of the trees waving from its backside. In the end, Hobart secured the aid of a friend and together they carried the trees the rest of the way, using an old ladder as a carrying platform. During the next few years Hobart watered the pines faithfully until they were able to persist on their own.

Unfortunately, these trees burned in the Coyote Fire, but in 1966 the Sierra Club took on the project of replanting the pines. On two February weekends 100 holes were dug and six-inch Aleppo pines were planted. Water was carried up from the creek in one-gallon containers throughout the spring, summer, and fall until the following rainy season.

Above the meadow the trail switches back and forth several times more to a point about 200 feet above the canyon floor. From there it levels for three quarters of a mile through chaparral shrubs that form a pleasant corridor. Then heads downhill to the creek and a cluster of bigleaf maple which seem to guard the entrance to the second of the Coldwater narrows. The walls are vertical and the sunlight generally indirect, as alder and maple crowns filter the sun's rays, creating a cool, verdant feeling. Along here are numerous spots to stop and relax and to sample the soothing sound of the brook as it splashes from boulder to boulder.

Continuing on through the narrows for a half mile more brings you to a large triangular meadow known as Tin Can Flat, for many years a familiar landmark. There, a small cabin was built by a man named William O'Connor. "The homesteading laws required that a dwelling be erected on each section," according to Public Historian Gregory King, so "O'Connor went into town, collected empty 5 gallon kerosene cans, flattened them, and had them carried back on a mule to a site he liked. There he put together a wood frame, and used the collected tin as the walls and roof. The floor was provided by Mother Nature—the ground."

Years later, adventurous boys used Tin Can Shack and it was even mentioned in several of the early-day guide books. But shortly after the 1925 earthquake a forest fire burned through the canyon and destroyed the structure.

County records show that a 160-acre section was also homesteaded below the Flat. John Stewart built a rough-hewn adobe on the side of a steep hill where he lived for several years. This changed in the 1920s when New York millionaire Ray Skofield moved to Santa Barbara and began to buy up the property in Rattlesnake Canyon, 456 acres in total, from Las Canoas Road to Tin Can Flat. He then started construction on a mansion overlooking the canyon, but the work ceased after the Depression began. Later the villa was developed into the Mt. Calvary Retreat.

Eventually the canyon was purchased by the City and County from Hobart Skofield, apparently for about half its value, under an agreement that its wilderness character would be maintained.

From the Flat, which marks the beginning of the Cozy Dell Shale, you can either follow the trail through the meadow, cross the creek to the east side, and hike three quarters of a mile up to Gibraltar Road or you can turn left and follow the connector trail up to its intersection with Tunnel Trail, which provides a full day's loop.

For those who are adventurous there are several other options available. After hiking to the upper end of the meadows, instead of continuing on up to Gibraltar Road, turn upstream. Shortly thereafter the stream enters a third set of narrows, this formed in the most dense of the mountain rock, Matilija Sandstone. The hike isn't easy, but the effort is rewarding. For a half mile there is a series of waterfalls and pools cascading one after the other down the slender channel.

Another way to return back downstream is to follow the creek rather than the trail from below the cluster of bigleaf maple down to the pine meadow. This isn't as difficult, though it is slower, and is especially rewarding for those who desire a bit more solitude and quiet than hiking on the trail sometimes offers.

Though most people don't realize it, there is also a trail on the east side of Rattlesnake Canyon which actually was the original trail. It is narrower and not as well maintained, now kept up by Jim Blakley, but it is abundantly shaded—more a tunnel through the chaparral than an opening—thus providing a touch of coolness on warm afternoons, and an enjoyable way to make a loop trip of your Rattlesnake Canyon hike. Rather than giving you explicit directions to the old trailhead, why not explore a bit yourself and see if you can't find it on your own?

COLD SPRINGS TRAIL— EAST FORK

**Intersection with Mountain Drive (752′) to intersection with
  East Camino Cielo (3400′)**
TOPO: Santa Barbara
DISTANCE: Four and one-half miles
ELEVATION GAIN: +2648 feet
GRADE: Steep

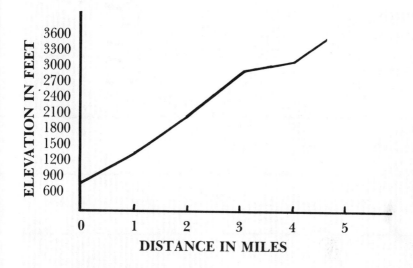

Cold Springs Trail was the first of the foothill trails I hiked many years ago and it is still my favorite. This is a creek that drops sharply through Coldwater and Matilija sandstones, with clear springs originating high above the trailhead, accessible only by an arduous but thrilling hike past the trail's end. Gushing forth from the shaly depths of the Juncal Formation, the creek runs cool and crisp year-round, flowing freely even on the hottest of August days.

The canyon beauty begins at road's edge. Alders thickly covered with green leaves flutter in the breeze and twenty yards upstream are the first pools. Even if you only have an hour, this is a place where you can enjoy a

few precious minutes of quiet. With the canyon walls and alder boughs for privacy, sandstone boulders for resting spots, and the creek's incessant babble for companionship, you'll fall in love with it, too.

The trail is reached by driving up Sycamore Canyon Road to Cold Springs Road. Turn north and drive past Westmont College to Mountain Drive and then a half mile east to the trailhead where the creek crosses the road in a shallow canal. The path immediately crosses to the east side of the stream and gradually rises through a forest of live oak before returning to the creek and a profusion of alder. In a thin opening, easily missed, is the turnoff to the West Fork trail.

"Yesterday Mr. Shedd and two men, two donkeys, and two mules came over from the Los Prietos mines by a new trail in less than eight hours, two of which were used to clear the trail of brush to the top of the mountain on the other side," the Santa Barbara newspaper reported on February 21, 1878, one of the earliest recorded accounts of the use of this trail.

Originally the trail followed not its present route up the East Fork but the West. Passing the site of the Cold Springs water tunnel, bored into the mountain on land donated by Eugene Sheffield, the trail led up to a 300-foot waterfall on the West Fork. There it switchbacked around it on the west and then proceeded nearby a large pointed rock at the top of the falls, named "The Pinnacle" by E.M. Heath in his 1904 book, *A Guide to Rides and Drives in Santa Barbara*. From there, it continued up the creek bottom through a narrows, then began to wind its way up shale slopes to the crest, where it crossed over and down the head of Gidney Creek to the Santa Ynez River.

As part of the establishment of the Santa Ynez Forest Reserve in 1899 the Cold Springs Trail was improved by the forest rangers. "It is considered advisable," Forest Inspector Louis A. Barrett wrote to his superiors in Washington in 1905, "to have one well built main trail crossing the Reserve from the Coast to the desert side and one half of the field force will be at work on this trail all the spring."

This route, however, was cut up the East Fork, as the Forest Service felt that the trail around the falls and up the shale slopes would be too difficult to maintain. With these improvements, the Cold Springs Trail became the main route over the mountain wall.

The East Fork heads away from the creek soon after the intersection with the West Fork and switches back and forth several times to a point giving a nice view of West Fork canyon, which was eroded laterally through the Cozy Dell Shale. From there the trail is level, but it is narrow and a bit dangerous unless you are careful, for the mountainside falls away rather precipitously. After a half mile it rejoins the creek, a lovely grouping of alders, and a small waterfall and pool.

There the trail crosses the stream and meanders back and forth to a number of pools and waterfalls. These open sandstone ledges and sunning spots are very popular for afternoon lunches. This also marks the end of the canyon section of the East Fork. A hundred yards beyond, the trail

turns right and rises up a strike canyon into the chaparral. Continue up the creek if you like. Though it rises rather steeply, the hike upcanyon is worthwhile. Many surprises await you if you have the energy to travel far enough.

Should you continue on the main trail, cross the creek and hike up the side canyon, also formed by the easily weathered Cozy Dell Shale. The path curves in a clockwise direction around the canyon and then winds up to a power line road which continues on to Hot Springs Canyon. Fifty yards along this road the upper section of the Cold Springs Trail begins on the left and rises quickly up into the Matilija Sandstone. A mile further up it crosses the flank of Montecito Peak, a thin cut across the solitary mountain which can be seen from the city, after which it curves through the Juncal Formation to the crest.

From there you can continue on down to the Santa Ynez River to a point just above Gibraltar Reservoir and Forbush Flat, another very picturesque overnight camping spot.

Should you wish to continue on down to the Hot Springs from the main trail, you'll find a side path about a half mile above the power lines that leads down to the springs.

COLD SPRINGS TRAIL—
WEST FORK

**Intersection with East Fork Trail (850′) to intersection with
Gilbraltar Road (1875′)**
TOPO: Santa Barbara
DISTANCE: Two miles
ELEVATION GAIN: +1025 feet
GRADE: Easy to Moderate

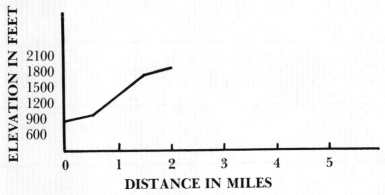

West Fork Trail is one of the nicest yet least known of the foothill trails. The lower canyon is extremely narrow, with solid bedrock over which the creek flows. The upper part opens into a large semi-circular valley, which is hidden from view until the last moment. Unlike most of the trails, which run in a north-south direction, the West Fork follows an east-west course. The reason for this can be found in the geology of this particular area.

North of the trail is Matilija Sandstone; to the south is Coldwater Sandstone. Sandwiched inbetween is Cozy Dell Shale. High along the crest the shale forms impressive saddles. As it dips across the ocean side of the Santa Ynez Mountains, it forms what are known as strike canyons, which flow at right angles to the main canyons. West Fork winds its way up the largest of these strike canyons.

Follow the directions for the East Fork trail until it intersects with the West Fork. Cross the creek and hike west, slowly climbing as the trail undulates up the left side of the narrow canyon. In the afternoon this section is shade-covered, making the hike pleasant on hot summer days.

The path wanders through dense green canyon vegetation for three quarters of a mile before opening into the valley. Slightly to right of center is a magnificent waterfall 200 to 250 feet high. Unfortunately, the main trail turns away from the falls at this point and rises quickly up the side of a large hill. A half mile later it connects with Gibraltar Road at a hairpin turn often used for target practice. Should you decide to hike to the road, take care, as those doing the shooting are often indiscriminate in their aim.

Most hikers do not realize that the West Fork watershed actually contains the main branch of Cold Springs Canyon. It lies in a hidden valley atop the large waterfall. The original trail over the crest followed this branch of the canyon, though the thick chaparral and the steep walls of Matilija Sandstone keep all but the most hardy from exploring its treasures.

After the Coyote Fire, according to Jim Blakley, the foremost authority on the Santa Barbara back country, remains of the old trail could be located. Carefully tracing his way along it, he was able to discover the homestead of a member of the Romero family, after which Romero Canyon is named. There he discovered a few relics left behind when the homestead was abandoned—the blade of a rusted plow, a few bottles, and a scattering of tin cans.

However, flood waters in 1969 washed much of this away, and the lack of fire since 1964 has allowed the chaparral to reclaim the land and to cover much of what remains of this history. Still, it is one of those places, so near to the city, that will remain a very special wilderness place because of the inhospitality of this part of chaparral country.

Should you decide to hike to the falls, or above, allow yourself plenty of time, and, just to be safe, let someone know where you have gone. From the main trail up the West Fork, a rough but serviceable path leads up to the base of the falls, though it is very steep. From there it is possible to work to the left, approximating the route of the historic trail, around "The Pinnacle", and back down to the top of the falls.

But again, take extreme care and allow ample time. I have participated personally in two overnight rescue operations with the Los Padres Search and Rescue Team because people underestimated their ability to find their way back down before sunset.

HOT SPRINGS TRAIL

End of Hot Springs Road (700') to Hot Springs (1350')
TOPO: Santa Barbara
DISTANCE: One and one-half miles
ELEVATION GAIN: +650'
GRADE: Moderate

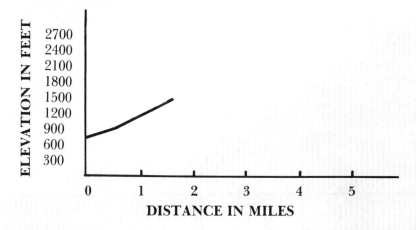

When Wilbur Curtiss came to Santa Barbara in the 1850s he was suffering from an incurable disease and doctors had given him only six months to live. Having lost his health in the mines, he was determined to spend his remaining days enjoying the scenery and wonderful climate in the Montecito hills.

One day while hiking in the foothills he noticed an old Indian, bathing in Hot Springs Creek, who seemed to be in remarkable health. An Indian boy who accompanied Curtiss on his daily excursions explained that the secret behind the old man's lengthy years, which totalled 110, was his bathing in some hot springs, which flowed from the base of a sandstone cliff further up the canyon.

After several hours of climbing, Curtiss reached the springs. There were four of these thermal pools, heated to 116 degrees, which contained sulphur, as well as arsenic, iron, magnesium, and other minerals. There he soaked himself in the soothing water and apparently even drank from one of the pools. Perhaps the hot springs had nothing to do with it, but after repeated visits to them, his health remarkably began to improve,

125

Photo courtesy Santa Barbara Historical Society

enough so that six years later, still alive and doing well, Wilbur Curtiss filed a homestead claim for this part of Hot Springs Canyon.

Slowly the site evolved as a resort-from camping spot to a tent camp, then a hut-before a cottage was eventually built. In 1873 the *Santa Barbara Morning Press* announced that a magnificent hotel costing $100,000 would be built at the mouth of the hot springs to accommodate the tourists flocking to the area. One writer boasted, "Many a rheumatic and neuralgic cripple has left his crutches here as a momento to the healing touches of the waters, and gone down from the rocky mountain glen out into the gay world, shouting praises to the boiling fountain which has invested him with new life."

By 1877 there was a large plunge, a shower, and three bath houses, each containing large tubs-enough in all to handle forty persons. In the early 1880s a three-story wooden hotel was finally completed on a bench above the springs. By this time Curtiss's original homestead had become the property of a number of wealthy Montecitans. Anyone with a bank account containing less than seven digits was not considered substantial enough to apply for membership to this private club.

In 1920, a forest fire destroyed much of the vegetation in the canyon and, with it, the hotel. It was rebuilt in 1923, but this time under the ownership of a corporation that contained but 17 members, all Montecito residents, who also controlled the Montecito Water Company. This structure, too, was destroyed, in the Coyote Fire of 1964. Though the land is still privately owned, it is now available to the less affluent of us.

The trailhead begins at the end of Hot Springs Road, about a half mile above Mountain Drive. There are several private driveways there, which may give you the impression that you have taken the wrong road. However, between the entries to these residences is a path marked by a small trail sign. The trail uphill parallels one of the asphalt driveways for 300 yards until the road turns to the left, and from this point on you are in the canyon proper. Continue up the canyon another quarter mile. There the trail turns right, dips, and crosses the creek and joins a dirt road, the old route up to the hot springs. Hike up the road for a hundred yards until you come to a side trail on the right, which meanders up into the chaparral. At this point you have two choices.

The road you are on continues somewhat steeply uphill for a mile to a point just below the site of the old hotel. There it joins a power line road. If you follow the power line to the left it will take you to the Cold Springs Trail. Another quarter mile up the main road is the ruins of the Montecito Hot Springs Club.

You can also reach the club by taking the side trail, a connector route to San Ysidro Canyon known as the McMenemy Trail which has a wooden trail sign marking its beginning. Follow it up a set of switchbacks to a prominent ridgeline formed by Coldwater Sandstone. These rocks provide ample opportunity for exploration or a relaxing place from which to watch the sunset, as they overlook all of Montecito. From there, the McMenemy Trail continues on down into San Ysidro Canyon.

Another path wanders through the sandstone boulders and continues up the ridgeline to the power line road. When you reach it, turn left and follow it for a half mile to the hot springs, which are located near the base of the Matilija Sandstone.

Along the way, as you pass the ruins, you can see remnants of the colorful past of this canyon: avocado trees, geraniums, and other plants not native to the area, such as a palm which marks an open grassy area. The main spring lies hidden on the west side of the creek about fifty yards from the ruins. The path to it is overgrown, but a little exploration will lead you to it.

A nice loop can be made by following the trail about a third of a mile beyond this spring, up to its intersection with the Cold Springs Trail. The overlook at the intersection gives an excellent view of the canyon and the ruins. From there, turn left and continue down the Cold Springs Trail to the power line trail and thence east back down to Hot Springs Canyon, or if you have left shuttle car at the Cold Springs trailhead, continue west down into Cold Springs Canyon.

SAN YSIDRO TRAIL

Intersection with Park Lane (500') to intersection with East
  Camino Cielo Road (3450')
TOPO: Carpinteria, Santa Barbara
DISTANCE: Four and one-half miles
ELEVATION GAIN: +2950 feet
GRADE: Moderate to Steep

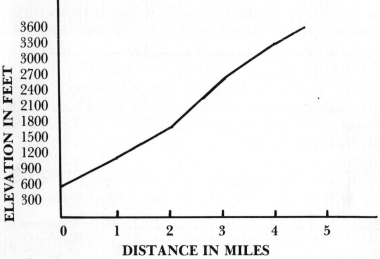

San Ysidro Creek, like Cold Springs, begins high in the Juncal Formation and thus flows late in the summer when other creeks are nearly dry. To reach the many pools and quiet rest spots, however, you must hike a mile upstream, until the canyon narrows enough and the trail comes close to the creek to have access to the many pools and quiet rest spots.

Oddly, the canyon is much narrower where it passes through the Cozy Dell Shale than below where it courses through the usually resistant Coldwater Sandstone. This is due to the peculiar nature of the geologic layers of the Santa Ynez Mountains which do not run parallel to the crest, but pass obliquely over the crest and then dip to the east across the mountains and under the coastal plain. The character of each layer changes as it descends from top to bottom.

For instance, when crossing the top of the mountains, Coldwater Sandstone crops out as intricately worn boulder fields, such as those at Lizard's Mouth or the Playground. Closer to Santa Barbara this sandstone angles down to form the Mission Crags and the magnificent toothed shape of Cathedral Peak. At lower elevation are the exquisite narrows at Seven Falls, and nearer the bottom those in Rattlesnake Canyon.

As it dips under the coastal flood plain, such as at San Ysidro Canyon, the sandstone is well eroded. This occurred during the Pleistocene, the period of rapid uplift, when the canyons were much deeper and continued farther seaward, perhaps as much as three miles.

★ ★ ★

From Santa Barbara the trailhead can be reached by taking the San Ysidro exit off of Highway 101. Turn north on San Ysidro Road and continue on it to East Valley Road. There turn right and follow East Valley one mile to Park Lane. Look for the eucalyptus-shrouded entrance to Park Lane just after crossing San Ysidro Creek and turn left onto it. In a half mile Mountain Drive enters from the left. Turn onto Mountain Drive and park near the horse corral fifty yards before a locked gate. When parking, please be considerate of those owning the houses and stables in the vicinity.

The trail begins to the right of a long driveway by a small sign which is marked with the San Ysidro Ranch brand and fastened to an oak tree. The path continues along the driveway for a hundred yards, then winds around the rear of a house and up onto a paved road. Follow this up to a wide dirt road that has a chain link gate partially across it and head up the dirt road. After a half mile you will come to a thick sequence of Coldwater Sandstone, the same rock that forms the scenic outcropping on the Hot Springs hike. Here the sandstone forms deep "V", the gateway to the inner canyon beyond.

Just before this "V", several connector trails lead off to the east and the west to join the canyons on either side of San Ysidro Canyon. To the east is the Pueblo Trail, which goes uphill rather sharply to cross over a ridgeline and down to upper Park Lane.

To the west is the McMenemy Trail which is marked by a sign. The trail crosses the creek and follows a small canyon up onto a grassy plateau above the San Ysidro Guest Ranch. From the meadow, several thin paths

radiate out, with the McMenemy again being noted by a small wooden trail sign. It goes up a depression behind a large hill west of the meadow.

The dirt road up the main canyon passes through the Gateway, a popular rock-climbing area, and continues uphill to a point where it is directly below the power lines. There it turns left, crosses the creek, and heads up to Hot Springs Canyon. Look for the beginning of San Ysidro Trail just before the turn. The trail wanders for one mile through canyon vegetation and oak woodland before heading up into the chaparral.

In the chaparral, the Cozy Dell Shale dominates, and this section is filled with small waterfalls, numerous pools, and many short paths leading down to picturesque spots for relaxing or picnicking. As you continue on, the canyon narrows and steepens as the trail passes into the Matilija formation. Along one section is a pipe railing to aid the climb upward, though it is hardly needed. You might also explore the creek through the narrows if you are adventurous enough to brave the rock scrambling and occasional willow thickets.

At the point where the creek branches, the trail turns northwest and steeply uphill and this marks the beginning of the Juncal Formation. This also marks the point at which you will no longer have access to water if you plan to continue up to the crest. If you want to keep this a relaxing, cool, and moderately easy hike, stop here. If you still have plenty of energy but don't want to leave the creek, try exploring the east fork. There is no trail, but the rock hopping is fun.

The trail to the crest has several switchbacks before it contours above the west fork for a half mile and then turns back to the east and a prominent ridgeline separating the two forks. Hiking to the crest adds another two miles, but the effort of making it to the top is well worth it.

From Camino Cielo, Cold Springs Trail is only a short distance to the west and it is tempting to make this a loop trip back down. Either follow the trail all the way into Cold Springs Canyon or when you get to the Hot Springs connector, follow it down to the springs for a soothing dip before catching the power line road east to San Ysidro Canyon.

San Ysidro Canyon shelters scores of other inviting destinations. I leave it to you to discover the 80-foot waterfall.

CHAPTER TEN

DRIVING THE CREST

Not all routes in the Santa Ynez Mountains begin in the foothills, nor do they all involve long hikes. For anyone who has driven along Camino Cielo and stopped for a few minutes of exploration, the rewards are self-evident. Though not everyone appreciates the subtle beauty of the chaparral, few would deny that the view from the crest is breathtaking. The drive in itself is a worthwhile way to spend a few afternoon hours.

The road along the crest was built during World War I. In October, 1916, the *Santa Barbara Daily News* announced that the Forest Service was planning to "open large sections of the forest reserve for lease in small tracts, large enough for a camping lodge and horse corrals, to entice many people to build camps in the woods next summer". To facilitate this, Congress approved $10,000,000 for the improvement of roads in the forest reserves.

The first was a rough road from San Marcos Pass to Los Prietos, which gave access to the upper Santa Ynez recreation area. On the ocean side of the mountains, spurred by the Forest Service activity and the urgings and financial support of private citizens, the County also contributed to opening the mountain wall.

One of the citizens to contribute most to this effort was George Owen Knapp, who had come to Santa Barbara in 1912. Born in 1855 in Hatfield, Massachusetts, Knapp graduated as a civil engineer from Rensselaer Polytechnic Institute of New York in 1876. He went on to work for People's Gas, Light and Coke Company in Chicago, building gas plants, and eventually became president of the company before moving on to Union Carbide, of which he was Chairman of the Board for 25 years.

Retiring in Santa Barbara, Knapp quickly became involved with everything that seemed to be identified with the city's progress, funding a nursing school at Cottage Hospital with a $200,000 contribution and donating substantial sums toward the construction of both All Saints-by-the-Sea Episcopal Church and Montecito Presbyterian Church. Pipe organs were a favorite of his and he also gave money for a number of them in other churches.

Next to building organs and hospitals, Knapp's abiding passion was building roads. Although he was past 60 years of age at the time, he personally supervised the construction of mountain roads to and from a lodge he was constructing in the Santa Ynez Mountains "with all the interest and enthusiasm of a man half his years". More than anyone, it was George Owen Knapp who was responsible for the construction of the route along the crest of the Santa Ynez Mountains.

From 1916 through the 1920s, as men like Knapp moved to Santa Barbara, ownership of the land in these mountains changed hands rapidly. The mountain setting was what drew the wealthy to the Santa

Ynez Mountains. It felt good to own a place at the top of the mountains with sweeping views, cool breezes, and unpolluted air, where "one could rub elbows with a historic past". Pioneer homesteaders gradually relinquished their holdings to "men with money, and [property] values hardly dreamed possible a few years ago for those sections were placed on the mountain properties".

Knapp himself built four palaces in the mountains: the "Castle" above Painted Cave, one by Wind Cave (it is likely that the steps at the Chumash cave there were built by him), a third near Refugio Pass, and the last in the upper Santa Ynez drainage, the site of the cement pool at Pendola Hot Springs, which was added by Knapp.

Some of the original mountain homesteaders began to move out. Homer Snyder, formerly a cook at the Arlington Hotel, had homesteaded his retreat originally for his ailing wife and subsequently developed his

Laurel Springs Ranch (now owned by Jane Fonda and Tom Hayden) as a vacation resort. Snyder sold a portion of his land to Knapp in 1916 for the mountain lodge, and in 1925 Knapp added Laurel Springs to his possessions. Others, such as Mike Finneran, the boisterous "Mayor of San Marcos Pass", died, and his land and that of a number of others passed on to properous Santa Barbarans.

Civilization was beginning to creep onto the mountaintop. Knapp and C.K. Billings, another lover of the mountains, hired laborers to remedy poor road conditions. Because of their efforts, horse trails were extended beyond the Pass east all the way to Ojai and west to Refugio Pass. In 1920, again due to Knapp's and Billings's efforts, San Marcos Pass Road was greatly improved. The two men provided half of the $50,000 expense for this work, the County the other half.

"Eventually these summit trails will be widened and graded for the automobile, giving Santa Barbara the finest system of scenic automobile roads in the state," prophesied the *Daily News* in 1917. Thus the mountains were opened, primarily because of the efforts of a dozen of Santa Barbara's riches citizens. For their work these men were praised highly, the *Daily News* stating, "They are strong advocates of the great out-of-doors, and under their leadership places in the wilds heretofore denied humans because of utter inaccessibility are being opened up to the hiker and the horseback rider."

If you would like to get the flavor of the old ridge road that Knapp and Billings helped build, take an afternoon and drive from San Marcos Pass to Refugio along West Camino Cielo. It is rough and bumpy, and there are lots of potholes and plenty of places for you to curse me for taking my advice, but it is well worth your time. Most likely you won't meet anyone on the entire 17-mile drive and you won't see sprawls of tract homes dotting the valley below. Only rarely will you see either Highway 101 or the Southern Pacific Railroad tracks. What you will see is a land that must be taken slowly and with care, as your springs and shocks will tell you.

As you drive beyond Lizard's Mouth and onto the dirt road a half mile beyond, you will switch back and forth down to a large saddle and into the rugged western portion of the Santa Ynez Mountains, where little has changed in the past 50 years.

KNAPP'S CASTLE

On April 9, 1916, George Owen Knapp purchased a 160-acre tract east of the Laurel Springs Ranch, wanting, in his words, "to make the tract a private mountain lodge that in natural beauty and grandeur will have few to equal it on the American continent." If the structure itself was anything like the view, it must have been awe-inspiring.

There were seven buildings in all, carved from thick sandstone blocks. The main house had five bedrooms, a large hallway, dining room, observatory, and a room especially designed for Knapp's pride and joy, a pipe organ. Over 20 men were employed during the construction of the lodge, which took more than four years. In addition to the main house, there was a studio next to it, a workman's cottage below, a dormitory

which housed six servants, and a superintendent's house in the hollow where the lower road forks away from the path leading up to the lodge.

Soon after the lodge was constructed, Knapp discovered a series of cascades in the canyon east of the lodge, known now as Lewis Falls. Shortly thereafter an automobile road led down to them. If you look closely after you have hiked down this road about a mile, you will see the faint remnants of the rock steps he had built to the base of the falls, now mainly a dirt path with sandstone rocks lining the way. There he also added a bath house and a pool fed by the falls, installed lighting to illuminate the falls at night, and even had the organ music piped all the way down from the house!

The music was provided by resident organist Dion Kennedy. Concerts were given at the rustic retreat from time to time by Kennedy as well as by invited guest artists of local and national repute, including Bruno Walter and Otto Klemperer.

Today all that remains of the Castle is the foundation and several chimneys rising like solitary spires into the sky. In 1940, Ms. Francis Holden purchased the lodge, but tragically five weeks later it was destroyed when a fire started in Paradise Canyon and raged out of control up the north slope of the Santa Ynez Mountains.

As the fire burned nearer, a friend of Ms. Holden painted the fiery mountain scene around her until she was forced to evacuate. Rather than worry about her fate, the woman seemed more concerned about her artwork, complaining of all the ashes falling in her paint and on her canvas. While everyone else panicked, including Ms. Holden, she calmly sat and painted.

The Forest Service finally made the women leave, with time enough only to throw a few belongings into a sheet, jump into a car, and go. When Ms. Holden tried to go back later to retrieve more, she was unable to get through a roadblock, though her chauffeur was able to climb a hill in time to see the flames reach the house and engulf it.

Five days later, only the observatory, built by Knapp in 1931 to house a large telescope, remained intact. Francis Holden never rebuilt, for the cost was simply too high. In 1964, the Coyote Fire claimed the observatory too, and the last of Knapp's dream.

Still, the beauty that Knapp saw as he first walked over the crest to his newly purchased property remains. Stepping onto the floor of the old observatory, its octagon-shaped walls long since destroyed, one can gain a vision of what life in the Santa Ynez Mountains must have been like a half century ago.

To visit the ruins, drive up Highway 154 and turn right onto East Camino Cielo. Continue for two miles (one mile past Painted Cave Road) to a prominent saddle with a locked Forest Service gate. Park there and hike the half mile down the driveway to the Castle. At one curve the silhouette of Knapp's Lodge comes into view. There is no more picturesque view of our pioneer heritage anywhere in the County.

BIBLIOGRAPHY

Bailey, Harry. *Weather of Southern California*. University of California Press. 1966.

Bakker, Elna. *An Island Called California*. University of California Press. 1971.

Blackburn, Thomas. *December's Child: A Book of Chumash Oral Narratives*. University of California Press. 1975.

Broughton, Jacqueline. *Santa Barbara's Native Wildflowers*. Santa Barbara Botanic Garden. 1977.

————— *Wildflowers of the Santa Barbara Region*. Santa Barbara Botanic Garden. 1958.

Collins, Barbara. *Key to Coastal and Flowering Plants of Southern California*. California State University Foundation. Northridge. 1972.

Dibblee, T.W., Jr. *Geology of the Central Santa Ynez Mountains, Santa Barbara County*. Bulletin 186. California Division of Mines and Geology. 1966.

Grant, Campbell. *The Rock Paintings of the Chumash*. University of California Press. 1965.

Hudson, Travis. *Guide to Painted Cave*. McNally and Loftin. 1982.

Hudson, Travis and Underhay, Ernest. *Crystals in the Sky: An Intellectual Odyssey Involving Chumash Astronomy, Cosmology and Rock Art*. Ballena Press. 1978.

Hudson, Travis and Blackburn, Thomas. *The Eye of the Flute: Chumash Traditional History and Ritual as Told by Fernando Librado Kitsepawit to John P. Harrington*. Santa Barbara Museum of Natural History. 1977.

Jaeger, Edmund, and Smith, Arthur. *Natural History of Southern California*. University of California Press. 1971.

Raven, Peter and Axelrod, Daniel. *Origin and Relationship of the California Flora*. University of California Press. 1978.

Santa Barbara Historical Society, *Noticias*. Quarterly Bulletin. *The Earthquake Issue*, Summer, 1959; *Mountain Wall Issue*, Fall, 1960; *Santa Ynez Valley Issue*, Autumn, 1962; *The Mountain Passes Issue*, Spring, 1964; *The Painted Cave Issue*, Fall, 1978.

Smith, Dick and Van Schaick, Frank. *California's Back Country: Mountains and Trails of Santa Barbara County*. McNally and Loftin. 1962.

Smith, Clifton. *A Flora of the Santa Barbara Region*. Santa Barbara Museum of Natural History. 1976.

Spaulding, Edward Seldon. *A Brief Story of Santa Barbara*. The Santa Barbara Historical Society. 1964.

———— *Camping In Our Mountains*. The Santa Barbara Historical Society. Undated.

———— *Santa Barbara, 1898-1925, As Seen By A Boy*. The Santa Barbara Historical Society. Undated.

Tompkins, Walker. *Goleta The Good Land*. Goleta Amvets Post No. 55. 1966.

———— *Stagecoach Days in Santa Barbara County*. McNally and Loftin. 1982.

Thompson and West. *History of Santa Barbara and Ventura Counties California*. Howell-North Books. 1961.

White, Stewart Edward. *The Mountains*. Hurst and Company. 1904.

NOTES

I would like to thank Kathy Malin for the care taken in editing my manuscript, and Bill McNally for giving me the freedom to revise *Day Hikes* without any restrictions. Without Kathy's many hours of help, and Bill's trust, the work would have been far less enjoyable and the final product less valuable.

I would also like to thank those who have spent so many hours with me in the mountains: Kevin, who is a very special friend; Wynne, who has always helped me keep the magic; Robin, who always encouraged me to follow my dreams; and especially Jim Blakley, who knows more about the Santa Barbara back country than anyone else, and who is always willing to share that knowledge.

Thank also to Stella Haverland Rouse for her *News Press* column, "Olden Days in Santa Barbara", which is the source of so many of the historical quotes.

I would also like to dedicate *Day Hikes* to the memory of Edward Seldon Spaulding, who died in 1982, but not before inspiring me to explore the Santa Ynez Mountains in great depth.

FOOTNOTES

Chapter 4

1. Hudson and Blackburn, *Eye of the Flute,* pp. 7 and 95.
2. Thanks to Bill Hyder, director of the Polis Lab at UCSB for his knowledge of Chumash rock art and his enthusiasm in transmitting it to others.
3. Johnny Flynn, Santa Barbara Bicentennial, "Stories of First People: Channel Coast Indian History," April 1, 1982.
4. For this section on the cultural evolution of the Chumash I am indebted to Steve Horne, author of the unpublished doctoral dissertation, *The Inland Chumash.*
5. The following section regarding the spirit world of the Chumash comes from "The Inland Chumash," a slide-tape presentation developed by Cary Sterling in 1979.

Chapter 5

1. Parfait, Michael, "The Back Country, A Place of Fundamentals," Santa Barbara Magazine, Fall 1977, pp. 6-8.

Chapter 8

1. *Noticias*, The Mountain Passes Issue, p. 1.
2. Fiske, Barbara, "The Arroyo Burro Litigation," Condor Call, December-January 1981.
3. Hufschmid, Brad, "A Historical Look at Santa Barbara's Changing Physical and Cultural Environment," unpublished paper, UCSB, 1983.
4. Tompkins, *Goleta The Good Land*, p. 20.
5. Brewer, William, *Up and Down California in 1960–1964*, pp. 46-47.
6. Thompson and West, *History of Santa Barbara and Ventura Counties*, pp 217-218.
7. King, Gregory, "La Cumbre Trail, Gone 50 Years, Still Used Daily," Condor Call, November 1982.